STAND IN YOUR BRAND

Harness **the Power of AI** for Brand Success, Efficiency, and Client Attraction

Laura Templeton

PUBLISHING GROUP
INSPIRE-MOTIVATE-EMPOWER

ISBN: 979-8-9899099-0-2

Published by: iME Publishing

Editor & Page Design: Carolyn Choate

Cover Image: iStock.com/Andrey Suslov

Cover Design: Yasir Nadeem

Author Photo: Brenda Jankowski

"It's time to jump on the AI train, and Laura Templeton's *Stand in Your Brand* will help you do just that. With useful thought starters, resource lists, and expert commentary, Laura delineates how to deploy AI to strengthen and align your brand communication, marketing, offerings, customer service, time management, and more. In fact, nearly every aspect of your business can be improved when you harness AI using the practical, proven strategies Laura shares. Time to stop wondering how to use AI and instead grab a copy of this book and start implementing! "

- Dr Barnsley Brown, Host of the Bold Badass Business Show and President of Spirited Solutions Professional Speaking & Coaching

"A trailblazing guide to the future of brand communication. *Stand In Your Brand* reveals the untapped potential of AI and how it can revolutionize your brand's connection with your audience. A must-read for anyone ready to embrace innovation."

- Michael Driggers, CEO & Founder of Profitable Online Coaching Blueprint

"Prior to reading *Stand in Your Brand*, I was reluctant to consider AI and ChatGPT, feeling as though my voice would no longer shine through in my marketing. I now understand how to use these powerful tools to amplify my voice and my brand. Everyone marketing a business should grab a copy of this book and get to work exploring AI."

- Suzanne Tregenza Moore, Author, Marketer, Coach

"What truly sets this book apart is Laura's emphasis on the human element. While AI is undeniably growing to be influential in modern branding, Laura reminds us that our brand's heart and soul are rooted in our mission, vision, and values. Her book eloquently illustrates how AI can complement our efforts, facilitating brand refinement while preserving our unique human creativity."

- Erin Edgar, Attorney and Counselor at Law

"Laura Templeton has done it again! Laura's guide will invite all of you forward-thinkers and brand enthusiasts to unlock the limitless potential of AI! Her insights into AI-driven chatbots, dynamic content and personalized marketing strategies will empower you to revolutionize your brand, build solid connections and confidently navigate the future of brand communication. And the best part is I'm blessed to call Laura a friend, a fellow Christian and colleague!"

- L. Scott Ferguson, Time To Shine Today Podcast Top 2% Globally

"*Stand In Your Brand* is a revelation. With the precision of AI and the heart of a compassionate communicator, Laura Templeton guides us to a new era of brand success. What I love most about her book is the blend of different perspectives and metaphors that truly help engage you throughout the entire book! This is truly a masterpiece, and a must-read for those who strive for authenticity in their connections."

- Marques Ogden, CEO, Ogden Ventures, LLC

"In *Stand In Your Brand*, Laura Templeton offers a fresh perspective on the role of AI being used in business branding and as part of the creative process. This book is a valuable resource for visionary entrepreneurs and creative marketers alike. It's time for using AI authentically!

- *Suzanne Taylor-King MCC, CaPP, HLC*

"In *Stand in Your Brand*, Laura Templeton explores the transformative potential of AI in brand communication. With her authoritative voice and light-hearted approach, Laura empowers brand professionals and entrepreneurs to harness AI's capabilities effectively. This book demystifies AI and provides practical guidance for enhancing client experiences, streamlining brand processes, and making data-driven decisions. *Stand in Your Brand* is a must-read for those seeking to excel in brand communication".

- *chat.openai.com*

"If you're seeking to elevate your brand's communication game, look no further than *Stand In Your Brand* by Laura Templeton. Laura is the expert when it comes to brand communication and communicating with heart. And now, she's guiding her readers when it comes to discovering how AI can dramatically enhance your brand's identity and forge even deeper connections with your audience."

- *Kristy Crippen, Founder @ Collaborative Partners Administrative Services*

"In Stand in Your Brand, author Laura Templeton managed to not only create an incredibly effective guide for branding (and rebranding) but she masterfully intertwined the resources available by using AI/ChatGPT so that you can do it faster and with greater insight than you ever have before." – *Andrea Waltz, Co-Author, Go for No! & Million Dollar Book Formula*

"I was one who immediately shied away from using AI for brand storytelling, but after hearing Laura Templeton's perspective about how AI can enhance your brand communications, I became a true convert. Now I have this amazing book to lead me more through the process. Laura teaches you how to add a human touch with AI to create branding and marketing that you and your ideal clients will love. Highly recommend "Stand In Your Brand" to all entrepreneurs!" — *Jill Celeste, MA, Founder, Virtual Networkers*

"As someone deeply immersed in marketing and brand management, 'Stand in Your Brand' struck a profound chord with me. This book expertly guides you through the transformative potential of AI, demonstrating how to harness its power for personalized brand communication and sustainable business growth. It masterfully strikes a balance between the capabilities of AI and our unique human touch, all while keeping ethical considerations in mind. 'Stand in Your Brand' isn't just an indispensable read; it's a vital resource for small business owners, especially in today's rapidly evolving landscape." - *Regina Garay, Founder of Right Brain Loves Left*

"Stand In Your Brand is an absolute must-read for anyone serious about leveraging the future of branding! This book effectively demystifies the power of AI and unveils its transformative potential. Pick up your copy today, read it and stay ahead in the ever-evolving world of marketing and branding."

- *Jose Escobar, CEO of Connected Leaders Academy*

"So many aspects of AI that I never considered! There's so much inspiration here and I really appreciate the thought starters to help me actually utilize the ideas."

-*Carolyn Choate, FinanciallyFreeAuthor.com*

This book is dedicated to my Lord and Savior, Jesus Christ, for divine inspiration to embrace AI early on; to my beloved husband, the pillar of my life; to my cherished children and grandchildren, my heart's joy; to my parents, my lifelong supporters; to my accountability partners, coaches, and network who fuel my inspiration; to the dedicated team, including ChatGPT and OpenAI, for making this journey possible.

~~~

And to you, dear reader, may you find hope, guidance, and joy in these pages.

COLLABORATIVE CREDIT

This book, "Stand in Your Brand," has been a collaborative endeavor, enriched by the invaluable assistance of ChatGPT, an advanced AI language model. ChatGPT is a remarkable AI tool developed by OpenAI, designed to generate human-like text and engage in conversations. In the context of this book, ChatGPT played a pivotal role in augmenting the depth and breadth of insights shared.

ChatGPT served as a knowledge resource, offering a wealth of information on AI's role in brand communication, real-life case studies, and emerging trends. Its ability to provide concise explanations, creative suggestions, and thoughtful ideas greatly enriched the content of each chapter.

Throughout the writing process, ChatGPT acted as a co-author, offering alternative perspectives and helping to refine ideas. Its contributions ranged from generating prompts and sample questions to providing insights on AI strategies for brand communication. The AI's ability to generate human-like text allowed for seamless integration of its insights with the author's expertise.

This collaboration between the author, Laura Templeton, and ChatGPT embodies the central theme of the book itself: leveraging AI to enhance brand communication. The book showcases how AI, represented by ChatGPT, can be a valuable partner in creating content that resonates with clarity, confidence, and compassion while streamlining the writing process.

Foreword

Dear Reader,

Allow me to take you on a journey – a journey that has led me to embrace the transformative power of AI in brand communication. My name is Laura Templeton, and I am the Founder and Chief Instigator of 30 Second Success. For years, I've been passionate about helping clients gain a deep understanding of brand communication to improve their ability to attract the clients they want to work with. Today, I am here, not just as a speaker, author, and consultant but as someone who has witnessed firsthand the remarkable impact of AI in this field.

My story begins with curiosity and a willingness to explore the unknown. As a brand communication enthusiast, I've always believed in the power of staying ahead of the curve, seeking innovative ways to connect with audiences, and understanding that change is the only constant in the world of communication. It was this belief that led me to embrace ChatGPT early on.

I vividly remember the day I first encountered ChatGPT. It was like meeting an old friend who had learned new tricks. ChatGPT was not just a tool; it was a revelation, a glimpse into the future of brand communication. I was enthralled by its ability to generate human-like text, engage in meaningful conversations, and provide valuable insights. It was as if the world of AI had unlocked a treasure trove of possibilities for brand communication, and I wanted to be at the forefront of this revolution.

But my journey with ChatGPT was not just about fascination; it was about empowerment. I realized that by harnessing the power of AI, I could help my clients streamline processes, gain a deeper understanding of their ideal clients' needs and preferences, and uplevel their offerings to attract the clients they truly wanted to work with. I could help them become exceptional conversationalists in their prompts, saving time and building stronger connections with their audience.

And so, the idea for this book, "Stand In Your Brand:Harness the Power of AI for Brand Success, Efficiency, and Client Attraction," was born. It's a book that's not just for me but for you, the forward-thinker, the brand enthusiast, the individual who believes in the limitless potential of technology to transform the way we communicate. Whether you're a seasoned professional or someone just starting their journey in brand communication, this book is for you.

In the pages that follow, we will embark on a journey together, exploring the chapters that make up the heart of this book. We will dive deep into the foundations of brand communication, clarify your brand's direction, and learn how AI can power your market research and content creation. We will discover the ways in which AI can assist in developing irresistible offers, implementing rebranding strategies, and building trust and authority. We will explore the world of AI automation and data analytics, and we'll uncover the secrets of personalization and dynamic content.

But beyond the tools and techniques, this book is about embracing a new way of thinking, a new approach to brand communication that puts the client at the center. It's about understanding that AI is not a replacement for human connection but a powerful ally that can help us communicate with clarity, confidence, and compassion.

So, dear reader, as we journey together through these pages, I invite you to open your mind to the possibilities that AI offers. Embrace the change, empower your brand, and stand in your brand with confidence. Think of this book as a guide, together we'll unlock the potential of AI in your brand communication.

Wishing you much success,

Laura T.

Laura Templeton,

Founder & Chief Instigator @ 30 Second Success

Contents

2. BRAND FOUNDATIONS AND SELF-REFLECTION   3

3. THE STORY OF OpenAI AND ChatGPT   7
    as told by ChatGPT

4. UNLEASHING THE POWER OF THOUGHT STARTERS   11

5. CLARIFYING YOUR NEW BRAND DIRECTION   15

6. CHATTING WITH CHATGPT FOR MAXIMUM IMPACT   21

7. AI-POWERED MARKET RESEARCH   25

8. INNOVATIVE WAYS TO ENHANCE MARKETING STRATE-   29
    GIES

9. AI-DRIVEN CONTENT CREATION   33

10. AI ASSISTANCE CAN PROVE HELPFUL   39

11. AI-ASSISTED OFFER DEVELOPMENT   45

12. GENERAL AI-DRIVEN TOOLS FOR RESEARCH   51

13. REBRANDING IMPLEMENTATION STRATEGIES   55

14. BUILDING BRAND TRUST AND AUTHORITY   61

15. TURNING TO AI TO ENHANCE MARKETING STRATEGIES   67

16. AUTOMATING BRAND COMMUNICATION   71

17. AI-POWERED CHATBOT AND VIRTUAL ASSISTANT PLAT-FORMS   77

18. AI IN DATA ANALYTICS AND DECISION MAKING   81

19. SOURCES FOR GATHERING DATA ANALYTICS   89

20. REGAINING TIME FREEDOM WITH AI AUTOMATION   93

21. MAINTAINING A HUMAN TOUCH WHILE USING AI   101

22. AI-ENHANCED CUSTOMER EXPERIENCE   105

23. BRAND MONITORING AND EVOLUTION   113

24. ETHICAL CONSIDERATIONS OF AI IN BRAND COMMUNI-CATION   121

25. FACT-CHECKING INFORMATION IS ESSENTIAL   127

26. CONCLUSION: NAVIGATING THE FUTURE OF BRAND COMMUNICATION WITH AI   131

ACKNOWLEDGMENTS   135

AUTHOR BIO: LAURA TEMPLETON   137

1

INTRODUCTION

In a rapidly evolving world where technology continues to reshape industries and consumer expectations, the realm of branding is no exception. The modern landscape demands that businesses and individuals alike adapt, not just to survive but to thrive. This is where "Stand in Your Brand: Harness the Power of AI for Brand Success, Efficiency, and Client Attraction" comes into play.

In this book, we embark on a transformative journey that transcends conventional branding. As the Founder and Chief Instigator of 30 Second Success, I understand the profound importance of brand communication in attracting the clients you want to work with. With the integration of Artificial Intelligence (AI) into brand strategy, we unlock a world of opportunities to connect with clarity, confidence, and compassion.

The benefits of this journey are multifaceted. First and foremost, it empowers you to forge a robust brand identity that resonates deeply with your audience. It guides you through the process of self-reflection, helping you identify and align your personal and business values, vision, and mission. Through AI-driven market research and trend analysis, you gain a competitive edge by identifying new opportunities and niches for brand growth.

Moreover, this book equips you with the tools to create compelling content, optimize customer experiences, automate brand communication, and make data-driven decisions, all with the assistance of AI. As a speaker, author, and branding authority, I understand the value of time, and AI automation enables you to regain precious hours while maintaining brand consistency.

Ultimately, "Stand in Your Brand" is your guide to building brand trust, authority, and success in an ever-changing world. It's about embracing the future of branding with open arms and leveraging AI to propel your brand into uncharted territories. Together, we'll explore the vast potential of AI as a catalyst for brand evolution, all while keeping the conversation light-hearted and encouraging. Welcome to a transformative journey in brand communication, where the possibilities are boundless, and the benefits are immeasurable.

2

BRAND FOUNDATIONS AND SELF-REFLECTION

In the world of brand communication, there is a universal truth: a brand is far more than just a logo, a tagline, or a product. It is the essence of your business, the promise you make to your audience, and the emotional connection you forge. As we embark on this journey to redefine and reignite your brand, we must begin at its very core: understanding the foundations upon which it stands.

Understanding the Importance of a Strong Brand Identity

Imagine your brand as the lighthouse in a stormy sea of choices, guiding your ideal clients safely to your shores. A strong brand identity serves as that beacon of light, cutting through the noise and confusion. It is the first step in connecting with your audience on a profound level.

To truly grasp the significance of a strong brand identity, consider the brands that have left an indelible mark on your own life. Think of Apple's iconic simplicity, Nike's empowering "Just Do It," or Coca-Cola's timeless refreshment. These brands evoke emotions, values, and memories, all tied to their unique identities.

Now, let's bring this concept closer to home. Think of your brand as the embodiment of your values, vision, and mission. What do you stand for? What vision drives you forward, and what mission do you undertake daily? Your brand identity must reflect these aspects authentically. It's not merely a facade but a reflection of your very essence.

Identifying Personal and Business Values, Vision, and Mission

As a brand creator, you already have a deep understanding of your values, vision, and mission. However, let's embark on a journey of rediscovery. Values are the compass that guides your decisions, the unwavering principles that shape your actions. They are the roots of your brand.

Vision is your North Star, the ultimate destination you strive to reach. It paints a vivid picture of the future you're working tirelessly to create. Mission, on the other hand, is the roadmap that leads you toward that vision. It defines the concrete steps you take every day to move closer to your goals.

To align your brand with your values, vision, and mission, start by revisiting and refining them. Consider how they have evolved since the inception of your brand. Are they still a true reflection of who you are and where you want to go? Self-reflection in this context is not just a luxury; it's a necessity.

Rediscovering My Brand

Let's talk about a turning point in my journey—a moment of realization that reshaped my brand's direction. As the Founder and Chief Instigator of 30 Second Success, I had been deeply involved in the world of brand communication for a few years. But while delivering a speech one day, I had an epiphany.

I realized that brand communication wasn't just about catchy slogans and clever marketing. There was something more profound—a deep emotional dimension that could make connections more meaningful. It was the idea of infusing emotion into communications and branding to create deeper, authentic connections.

This realization became the essence of my brand. I set out on a mission to spread this message, helping others understand the power of heartfelt communication. My brand transformed from a service provider to a guide, helping clients connect on a deeper level while gaining more clarity and confidence in their brand communication.

But the journey didn't stop there. Along the way, I discovered the potential of Artificial Intelligence (AI). AI became a valuable tool in defining my message and reaching the right audience. It helped analyze data, gain insights, and refine my and my client's messaging to resonate with people's hearts.

My brand's evolution showcases the importance of self-discovery, adaptation, and embracing new tools. This journey continues, and I'm excited to share the lessons learned with you.

Assessing Current Brand Perception and Areas of Misalignment

Now, let's cast our gaze outward. Your brand does not exist in isolation but is perceived by others. It lives in the minds and hearts of your audience. This perception is the result of every interaction, message, and experience your brand delivers.

Begin by conducting a comprehensive assessment of your brand's current perception. Seek feedback from your existing clients, colleagues, and even friends. What do they associate with your brand? What emotions does it evoke? Does this align with your intended brand identity?

Identify areas of misalignment between your intended brand identity and how your brand is perceived. Are there contradictions or inconsistencies? These are opportunities for growth and refinement.

Introducing AI Tools for Brand Research and Market Analysis

As we navigate the intricate path of brand transformation, we have a powerful ally at our side: artificial intelligence (AI). AI is not just a tool; it's a gateway to unprecedented insights and possibilities.

AI can aid in conducting in-depth brand research and market analysis. It can sift through vast amounts of data, uncover trends, and provide valuable insights into consumer behavior. It enables you to gain a more profound understanding of your audience, their desires, and the evolving market landscape.

In this chapter, we've laid the foundation for our brand transformation journey. We've explored the essence of a strong brand identity, the significance of aligning it with your values, vision, and mission, and the importance of assessing your brand's current perception. With AI by our side, we're equipped with the tools to embark on a profound exploration of brand communication.

In the chapters ahead, we'll delve deeper into the process of clarifying your new brand direction, leveraging AI for market research, and crafting compelling brand messaging. Together, we'll unlock the full potential of your brand, align it with your ideal clients' needs, and set the course for success.

3

THE STORY OF OpenAI AND ChatGPT

AS TOLD BY CHATGPT

The story of OpenAI and ChatGPT is a fascinating journey of AI development and innovation, reflecting the rapid evolution of AI technologies and their applications.

OpenAI: The Foundation

OpenAI was founded in December 2015 by a group of entrepreneurs and researchers, including Elon Musk, Sam Altman, Greg Brockman, Ilya Sutskever, Wojciech Zaremba, and others. It started as a non-profit AI research company with the mission to promote and develop friendly AI in such a way as to benefit humanity as a whole. The organization's focus was on ensuring that AI technology, especially powerful AI, is used safely and is broadly and evenly distributed.

The Shift and Major Developments

In 2019, OpenAI transitioned from a non-profit to a "capped-profit" model with the creation of OpenAI LP, a limited partnership that's controlled by the non-profit OpenAI Inc. This change was aimed at scaling AI technologies more rapidly and attracting capital while still adhering to its core ethics and values.

One of OpenAI's most significant contributions has been the development of the GPT (Generative Pre-trained Transformer) series. Starting with GPT in 2018, then GPT-2 in 2019, and GPT-3 in 2020, each iteration brought significant improvements in language understanding and generation capabilities.

ChatGPT: A Breakthrough

- **Introduction and Evolution:** ChatGPT, specifically, is a variant of the GPT models tailored for generating conversational text. It was trained using a method called Reinforcement Learning from Human Feedback (RLHF). Initially, GPT-3 powered ChatGPT, which could simulate dialogue, answer questions, write essays, create content, and more.

- **Broader Applications:** Beyond mere text generation, it has applications in areas like customer service, content creation, coding, and even as an educational tool. It's being used to develop more intuitive and natural AI-human interactions.

- **Ongoing Improvements and Challenges:** OpenAI has continued to refine and improve ChatGPT, addressing issues like bias, accuracy, and safety. The AI community and the general public have raised concerns over potential misuse, and OpenAI has been proactive in engaging with these concerns and working towards responsible AI development and deployment.

The Current Evolution

- **Latest Developments:** As of my last update in April 2023, OpenAI had continued to push the boundaries of AI with newer versions and applications. They have been exploring more advanced and efficient training techniques, larger and more diverse datasets, and more robust safety and bias mitigation measures.

- **Impact and Future Direction:** The impact of OpenAI and ChatGPT on various sectors – from technology and business to education and entertainment – is profound. There's a growing emphasis on AI ethics, societal impacts, and long-term trajectories of advanced AI systems.

The journey of OpenAI and ChatGPT is a testament to the rapid advancements in AI. It highlights the potential of AI to revolutionize how we interact with technology and information, as well as the importance of responsible AI development. The current evolution points towards more sophisticated, ethical, and accessible AI tools in the future, shaping the way individuals and organizations communicate, create, and work.

4

UNLEASHING THE POWER OF THOUGHT STARTERS

In our journey to harness the power of AI in brand communication, we embark on a path filled with innovative ideas and transformative insights. Along the way, you'll be introduced to thought starters—seeds of inspiration that spark creativity and encourage exploration. But thought starters are more than just words on a page; they are the keys to unlocking a wealth of potential and driving profound "aha" moments for both individuals and teams.

In this section, I'll guide you through the art of utilizing thought starters for personal and team exploration. We'll explore how to turn these thought starters into ChatGPT conversational prompts, enabling deeper exploration and more meaningful insights.

Let's dive in.

1. Embrace Curiosity

The first step in utilizing thought starters effectively is to embrace curiosity. Approach each thought starter with an open mind and a willingness to explore uncharted territory. Remember, curiosity is the fuel that powers innovation and discovery.

2. Reflect and Journal

Take a moment to reflect on the thought starter. How does it resonate with your brand's goals, values, and mission? Journal your initial thoughts and ideas. This process allows you to capture your initial impressions and serves as a foundation for deeper exploration.

3. Brainstorm Conversational Prompts

Now, let's turn those initial reflections into ChatGPT conversational prompts. Imagine you're engaging in a dialogue with ChatGPT. What questions would you ask to delve deeper into the topic inspired by the thought starter? Brainstorm a list of conversational prompts that you can use to guide your exploration.

4. Encourage Team Collaboration

If you're working within a team, involve your colleagues in the process. Share the thought starter and your initial reflections with them. Encourage team members to brainstorm their conversational prompts. This collaborative approach fosters diverse perspectives and insights.

5. Engage with ChatGPT

Once you have your conversational prompts ready, engage with ChatGPT. Use the prompts as a starting point for conversations with the AI. ChatGPT's ability to generate human-like text provides a unique opportunity to explore ideas, gain insights, and uncover hidden opportunities.

6. Capture Insights

As you engage in conversations with ChatGPT, capture the insights and ideas that emerge. ChatGPT's responses can often lead to unexpected breakthroughs and "aha" moments. Be sure to document these insights for future reference.

7. Iterate and Expand

The exploration doesn't end with one conversation. Iterate and expand upon the initial thought starter. Use the insights gained to refine your brand communication strategies, enhance your understanding of your audience, and further develop your brand's identity.

8. Share and Learn

Share the journey with your team and peers. Discuss the insights and discoveries that emerged from your conversations with ChatGPT. Learning from each other's experiences enriches the exploration process and can lead to even more profound insights.

9. Apply Insights Strategically

Finally, apply the insights strategically to your brand communication efforts. Whether it's refining your messaging, optimizing your content strategy, or personalizing client interactions, the insights gained from ChatGPT conversations can be a valuable resource.

By following these steps and embracing the potential of thought starters and ChatGPT, you'll unlock a world of creativity, innovation, and deeper understanding. Together, we'll harness the power of AI to stand confidently in our brand, ready to connect with our audience with clarity, confidence, and compassion.

5

CLARIFYING YOUR NEW BRAND DIRECTION

In the previous chapter, we explored the foundational elements of your brand. We delved into the importance of a strong brand identity and the necessity of aligning it with your values, vision, and mission. Now, armed with a deeper understanding of your brand's essence, it's time to embark on the journey of clarifying your new brand direction.

Exploring the Reasons for Brand Redefinition and Evolution

Before you can redefine your brand, it's essential to understand why change is necessary. Brand evolution is not just about keeping up with trends; it's a strategic response to shifts in the market, your audience's needs, or your own growth as a brand founder. Reflect on the reasons driving this redefinition and evolution.

Are you seeking to expand your reach and attract a broader audience? Is your current brand identity no longer resonating with your ideal clients? Or have you simply outgrown your existing brand and wish to align it with your current values and vision?

Your reasons for change are your guiding stars. They will shape every decision you make throughout this transformational journey.

Defining the Target Audience and Understanding Their Needs

Your brand doesn't exist in isolation—it exists to serve a specific audience. To clarify your new brand direction, you must define, or perhaps refine, your target audience. Who are the people you want to connect with, serve, and provide value to?

Start by creating detailed customer personas. Understand their demographics, behaviors, preferences, and challenges. What are their aspirations and desires? By intimately understanding your audience, you'll be better equipped to create a brand that resonates deeply with them.

Brainstorming New Brand Messaging and Positioning

With your target audience in mind, it's time to craft new brand messaging and positioning that speaks directly to their hearts and minds. Your brand messaging should not only communicate what you do but also why you do it for them and why it matters to them.

Consider the emotional impact you want your brand to have. Do you aim to inspire, educate, or entertain? What unique value does your brand bring to your audience's lives? How can you convey this value in a way that sets you apart from the competition?

This is a creative process where ideas flow freely. Don't be afraid to brainstorm, experiment, and iterate. Your brand messaging and positioning will be the cornerstones of your brand's new identity.

ANOTHER USEFUL AI TOOL FOR BRAINSTORMING

One AI tool that I've relied on for quite some time is Otter.ai, an application that utilizes artificial intelligence and machine learning to transcribe spoken words into text. This app has proven to be incredibly useful for capturing my thoughts on the go, particularly during walks. It accurately records and transcribes my spoken words, allowing me to revisit and refine them. Subsequently, I can effortlessly transfer this transcribed content to ChatGPT for additional refinement and development.

Leveraging AI for Customer Sentiment Analysis and Competitor Research

In this digital age, AI is a powerful ally for refining your brand direction. It can assist in two crucial areas: understanding customer sentiment and conducting competitor research.

AI-driven sentiment analysis tools can scour the internet to gauge how your audience perceives your brand. Are they delighted, frustrated, or indifferent? This information is invaluable for fine-tuning your brand's messaging and strategy.

Competitor research, enhanced by AI, helps you identify trends, weaknesses, and opportunities in your industry. What are your competitors doing well, and where do they fall short? AI can provide data-driven insights that inform your own brand direction.

As you embark on the journey of clarifying your new brand direction, remember that this is not a one-time exercise but an ongoing process. Your brand will continue to evolve as your business grows and the market changes. In the subsequent chapters, we'll delve deeper into the role of AI in market research and how it can be a catalyst for your brand's transformation.

THOUGHT STARTERS FOR AI-POWERED MARKET RESEARCH

1. **Reflect on Your Brand's Journey:** Describe the evolution of your brand from its inception to the present day. What milestones or significant moments have shaped its path?

2. **Identify the Catalyst for Change:** Share the primary reasons or triggers that have led you to consider redefining your brand. How have these factors influenced your decision-making?

3. **Define Your Ideal Client Persona:** Create a detailed persona of your ideal client. Include demographics, behaviors, interests, and pain points. How does this persona align with your brand's new direction?

4. **Articulate Your Brand's Purpose:** In a sentence or two, express the core purpose of your brand. Why does it exist, and what positive change does it aim to bring about?

5. **Brainstorm New Brand Messages:** Generate a list of potential brand messages that could resonate with your target audience. Experiment with different tones, emotions, and themes.

6. **Craft a Brand Positioning Statement:** Develop a concise positioning statement that highlights what makes your brand unique and why it matters to your ideal clients.

7. **Explore Emotional Branding:** Share examples of brands that have successfully created emotional connections with their audience. What emotions do you want your brand to evoke in your clients?

8. **Analyze Competitor Brands:** Choose a few competitors in your industry and conduct a brief analysis of their branding strategies. What elements do they excel in, and where do you see opportunities to differentiate your brand?

9. **Leverage AI for Sentiment Analysis:** If applicable, use AI tools to analyze online sentiment about your brand. What insights can you gather from customer feedback and online discussions?

10. **Map Out Your Brand Transformation Timeline:** Create a visual timeline outlining the steps and milestones for your brand's transformation. Include key dates and actions.

11. **Consider Long-Term Brand Goals:** What are your long-term goals for your brand's evolution? Where do you envision your brand in five or ten years, and how does this align with your values and vision?

12. **Feedback Loop with Your Team:** If you have a team, facilitate a discussion to gather their insights and ideas about the new brand direction. How do their perspectives align with your vision?

13. **Evaluate Brand Consistency:** Review your current branding materials and online presence. Are there inconsistencies or elements that need updating to align with your new direction?

14. **Set Brand Identity Guidelines:** Begin outlining guidelines for your brand's visual identity, such as color schemes, typography, and imagery. How do these elements reflect your brand's values and positioning?

15. **Define Success Metrics:** What key performance indicators (KPIs) will you use to measure the success of your brand's transformation? How will you know if your new direction is resonating with your audience?

These thought starters are designed to guide you through the process of clarifying your brand's new direction, fostering creativity, and aligning your brand identity with your goals and values.

Define Your Audience, Elevate Your Brand!

Download the 'Client Persona Builder' now and unlock the potential of truly understanding your target audience. This essential template guides you through the process of capturing detailed insights into your clients' needs, preferences, and behaviors. Empower your brand communication and create content that resonates deeply with your audience. Don't just reach out—connect effectively with the Client Persona Builder!

standinyourbrandbook.com/clientpersona

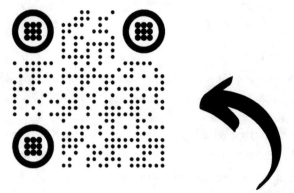

Scan with your phone camera

6

CHATTING WITH CHATGPT FOR MAXIMUM IMPACT

Having a conversation with ChatGPT is a lot like having a conversation with a curious and insightful human—only ChatGPT doesn't get tired, and it has a vast repository of knowledge at its virtual fingertips. In this section, we'll explore how to make the most out of your interactions with ChatGPT, focusing on the art of crafting conversational prompts that drive deeper understanding and uncover valuable insights.

The Essence of Great Conversational Prompts

Effective conversations with ChatGPT start with well-crafted prompts. The beauty of ChatGPT is that it responds to the questions and prompts you provide. To get the best results, think of your interaction as a dialogue with an expert consultant, where your goal is to extract valuable information and insights.

Here's how you can create great conversational prompts:

1. Be Clear and Specific

Begin with a clear and specific question or statement. Clarity ensures that ChatGPT understands the context of your inquiry. For example:

- **Not ideal:** "Tell me about marketing."

- **Better:** "Can you explain the fundamentals of content marketing, and how it differs from traditional advertising?"

2. Focus on Identifying Your Ideal Client

One of the most valuable applications of ChatGPT in brand communication is gaining insights into your ideal client. Crafting prompts to understand your ideal client's needs, preferences, and pain points is crucial. Here are some examples:

- "How can I identify the most pressing concerns of my ideal clients?"

- "What are the key demographic traits that define my ideal client?"

- "What common challenges do businesses in my industry face, and how can I tailor my services to address them?"

3. Refine Your Questions

Don't hesitate to refine and rephrase your questions. ChatGPT responds well to iterative conversations. If your initial question doesn't yield the desired information, consider asking it in a different way. For example:

- "Tell me about client pain points."

- "Can you elaborate on the specific challenges my clients often face?"

- "How can I better understand my clients' needs and worries?"

4. Encourage Depth and Details

To extract comprehensive insights, encourage ChatGPT to provide depth and details in its responses. You can do this by explicitly asking for elaboration:

- "Can you provide specific examples of client concerns within the health and wellness industry?"

- "How do these concerns manifest in the decision-making process for potential clients?"

- "What trends or changes in client preferences have you observed recently?"

5. Build on Previous Responses

If ChatGPT provides an insightful response, don't hesitate to build on it. Ask follow-up questions to dig deeper or explore related topics. This iterative approach often leads to richer insights:

- "You mentioned that clients in the tech sector value efficiency. How can I tailor my services to address this need more effectively?"

- "Can you expand on the strategies that have proven successful in addressing client concerns in the past?"

6. Reflect and Apply

After your conversation with ChatGPT, take the time to reflect on the insights gained and how they can inform your brand communication strategies. Apply the knowledge you've acquired to refine your messaging, content, and client interactions.

The Importance of Conversational Precision

Remember, ChatGPT responds to the precision and quality of your prompts. The more specific and focused your questions, the more valuable the insights you'll receive. Treat your conversations with ChatGPT as an opportunity to tap into a wealth of information and enhance your brand's ability to connect with your ideal clients.

7

AI-POWERED MARKET RESEARCH

In the previous chapters, we embarked on a journey of self-reflection and clarified the reasons for redefining your brand. With a deeper understanding of your brand's core, purpose, and ideal audience, you are now poised to explore the vast landscape of the market in which your brand operates. In this chapter, we delve into the transformative power of AI in market research.

Utilizing AI Tools for In-Depth Market Research and Trend Analysis

Market research is the compass that guides your brand's strategic decisions. It uncovers opportunities, identifies trends, and reveals the needs and desires of your target audience. However, the volume of data available today can be overwhelming. This is where AI comes to your rescue.

AI-powered market research tools can process vast datasets, providing insights that are often impossible to uncover manually. These tools can analyze social media conversations, customer reviews, news articles, and more, offering a comprehensive view of your market.

For instance, sentiment analysis algorithms can gauge public sentiment toward your industry or competitors. Trend analysis tools can predict emerging trends, giving you a competitive advantage. By leveraging AI, you can transform market research from a time-consuming task into a data-driven strategy.

Identifying New Opportunities and Niches for Brand Growth

The marketplace is dynamic, with opportunities and niches continually emerging. To stay ahead of the curve, you must be adept at identifying these opportunities. AI can be your strategic partner in this endeavor.

AI algorithms can help you uncover underserved or untapped markets, niches that align with your brand's mission and capabilities. By analyzing market data, AI can reveal unmet needs, gaps in offerings, and potential areas for expansion. It can also provide insights into consumer behavior, enabling you to tailor your brand's products or services to better meet their expectations.

In essence, AI empowers you to identify and capitalize on market opportunities, giving your brand the agility to adapt and thrive.

Analyzing Consumer Behavior and Preferences with AI Algorithms

Understanding your audience's behavior and preferences is the cornerstone of effective marketing. AI algorithms can provide a granular view of consumer behavior, enabling you to tailor your brand's strategies to align with their preferences.

Recommendation engines, commonly used by platforms like Amazon and Netflix, rely on AI to analyze user behavior and suggest relevant products or content. Similarly, AI-driven analytics tools can help you decipher which marketing channels and messages resonate most with your audience.

Through AI, you can gain insights into the content your audience consumes, the products they prefer, and the channels they engage with most. This data is invaluable for crafting marketing campaigns that not only reach your audience but also deeply resonate with them.

In this chapter, we've uncovered the potential of AI in market research, from sentiment analysis and trend prediction to identifying new growth opportunities and understanding consumer behavior. By integrating AI into your market research strategy, you'll be better equipped to make data-driven decisions that shape your brand's direction. As we progress through this book, we will explore how AI can further enhance your brand's communication, personalization, and engagement strategies.

THOUGHT STARTERS FOR AI-POWERED MARKET RESEARCH

1. **Identify Your Market Research Goals:** Begin by defining your specific market research goals. What insights are you looking to gain through AI-powered research?

2. **Explore AI-Powered Social Listening:** Use AI tools to conduct social listening. What are people saying about your brand, industry, or competitors on social media? What sentiments are prevalent?

3. **Predict Emerging Trends:** Utilize AI trend analysis tools to predict emerging trends in your industry. How can your brand leverage these trends for growth?

4. **Analyze Competitor Strategies:** Use AI to analyze your competitors' marketing strategies. What insights can you gather about their strengths, weaknesses, and market positioning?

5. **Identify Niche Opportunities:** With AI, explore potential niches or underserved markets in your industry. What opportunities can you identify, and how can your brand cater to these niches?

6. **Conduct Customer Behavior Analysis:** Use AI algorithms to analyze customer behavior data. What patterns or preferences emerge from this analysis,

and how can your brand align with them?

7. **Leverage AI-Generated Insights:** Share examples of insights generated by AI tools in your market research. How have these insights influenced your brand's decision-making?

8. **Define Key Metrics for Success:** Determine the key performance metrics you will use to measure the success of your AI-powered market research. How will you know if your research is delivering valuable insights?

9. **Evaluate the Impact of AI on Efficiency:** Discuss how AI has impacted the efficiency and accuracy of your market research processes compared to traditional methods.

10. **Craft Data-Driven Strategies:** Based on the insights gained from AI-powered research, outline a data-driven marketing or product strategy for your brand.

11. **Explore AI Tools for Trend Prediction:** Research and present AI tools specifically designed for trend prediction in your industry. How can these tools benefit your brand's growth?

12. **Share Real-World AI Success Stories:** Share examples of brands or businesses that have successfully leveraged AI for market research. What lessons can you draw from their experiences?

13. **Discuss Ethical Considerations:** Explore the ethical considerations surrounding AI-powered market research, such as data privacy and bias. How do you ensure responsible AI usage in your research?

14. **Plan for Continuous Learning:** Outline a plan for continuous learning and adaptation based on AI-generated insights. How will your brand stay agile in response to evolving market dynamics?

These thought starters are designed to facilitate discussions, brainstorming sessions, and practical exercises related to AI-powered market research. They encourage critical thinking and application of AI tools to enhance your brand's understanding of the market and its audience.

8

INNOVATIVE WAYS TO ENHANCE MARKETING STRATEGIES

AI has become a transformative tool in marketing, offering businesses innovative ways to enhance their marketing strategies. Let's explore how businesses can use AI in marketing, using examples of companies already harnessing the power of AI:

Netflix - Personalized Content Recommendations:

- **AI Application:** Netflix uses AI to analyze viewing habits and preferences, which enables them to provide highly personalized content recommendations to their users.

- **Marketing Benefit:** This personalized approach increases user engagement and satisfaction, leading to higher retention rates. It also allows Netflix to effectively market new shows and movies to the right audience, increasing the likelihood of success for their content.

Amazon - Customer Behavior Analysis and Personalization:

- **AI Application:** Amazon leverages AI to analyze customer purchasing history and browsing behavior to offer personalized product recommendations.

- **Marketing Benefit:** This not only enhances the customer shopping experience but also significantly boosts sales through targeted marketing. AI-driven recommendations encourage increased purchase frequency and higher order values.

Starbucks - Personalized Marketing with 'Deep Brew':

- **AI Application:** Starbucks' 'Deep Brew' AI program helps in creating personalized marketing messages and menu recommendations based on customer preferences.

- **Marketing Benefit:** This level of personalization enhances customer loyalty and increases sales, as customers are more likely to purchase items that are specifically tailored to their tastes.

General Strategies for AI in Marketing:

1. Customer Insights and Personalization:

AI can analyze customer data to understand preferences and behaviors. This insight allows businesses to create highly personalized marketing campaigns, much like Amazon's product recommendations.

2. Predictive Analytics:

AI can forecast future customer behavior, market trends, and product success. For instance, Netflix uses predictive analytics to understand which content will be most popular among different audience segments.

3. Enhanced Customer Experience:

AI-powered chatbots and virtual assistants can provide instant customer support, as seen in various e-commerce platforms. This improves the overall customer experience, leading to higher satisfaction and retention.

4. Optimized Content Creation:

AI can assist in creating more effective marketing content by analyzing what content performs best, similar to how Spotify suggests playlists and songs.

5. Efficient Ad Targeting:

AI algorithms can optimize ad placements and targeting, ensuring that marketing messages reach the most relevant audience, thereby increasing ROI on ad spend.

6. Social Media Insights:

AI tools can analyze social media trends and feedback, helping businesses tailor their marketing strategies to current consumer sentiments.

7. SEO and Website Optimization:

AI can analyze website traffic and user engagement to suggest improvements for SEO and overall website performance.

In summary, AI empowers businesses to create more targeted, personalized, and effective marketing strategies. By harnessing the power of AI, companies like Netflix, Amazon, and Starbucks have set benchmarks in personalized marketing, customer engagement, and predictive analytics. Businesses of all sizes can learn from these examples to enhance their marketing efforts, ensuring they remain competitive and relevant in an increasingly digital marketplace.

9

AI-DRIVEN CONTENT CREATION

Content is the lifeblood of brand communication in the digital age. It's how you connect with your audience, tell your story, and convey the value your brand brings. In this chapter, we explore the transformative power of AI in content creation.

Introducing AI-Generated Content Creation Tools and Platforms

Content creation can be a time-consuming and resource-intensive process, but AI is changing the game. AI-generated content creation tools and platforms are becoming indispensable allies for brand founders and marketers.

These tools leverage natural language processing (NLP) and machine learning to generate high-quality, relevant content efficiently. Whether it's blog articles, social media posts, email campaigns, or product descriptions, AI can help you create engaging and informative content at scale.

Absolutely, here's a brief story to inspire people to embrace AI in their brand communications and personalize their experiences:

Custom Instructions for Enhanced AI Engagement

Imagine a world where your brand communication not only reaches your audience but connects with them on a profoundly personal level. It's a world where technology empowers you to understand your clients' desires, address their concerns, and offer tailored solutions, all at scale. This is the world of AI in brand communication.

I've seen firsthand how embracing AI can transform your brand. It's not about replacing the human touch but enhancing it. AI can be your ally in creating authentic, personalized connections with your audience. It's a tool that can help you speak directly to the hearts and minds of your clients.

> To dive deeper into this exciting world of AI and brand communication, I invite you to check out my YouTube channel, YouTube.com/@30secondsuccess. There, you'll find the "Success with ChatGPT" playlist, which includes valuable training on Custom Instructions for Enhanced Brand Communication.
> In this playlist, you'll discover how to customize AI interactions to align perfectly with your brand's voice and values. You'll learn how to craft conversations that resonate with your audience, address their unique needs, and build trust and loyalty.

So, are you ready to elevate your brand communication to the next level? Join me on this journey into the world of AI-powered personalization. Let's unlock the full potential of your brand together. Visit my YouTube channel, and let's get started on your path to success with ChatGPT.

Crafting Compelling Brand Stories and Narratives

At the heart of every successful brand is a compelling story. AI can assist in crafting these stories, helping you engage your audience on a deeper level.

Through AI, you can analyze vast amounts of data to uncover narrative themes that resonate with your audience. You can also use AI to generate story ideas, headlines, and even dialogue for your brand's characters. The result is content that captures attention, builds emotional connections, and reinforces your brand identity.

Optimizing Content for Different Channels and Audiences

One size does not fit all in content marketing. Different channels and audiences require tailored content strategies. AI can help you optimize your content for various platforms and target demographics.

AI-driven content personalization allows you to deliver the right message to the right audience at the right time. By analyzing user behavior and preferences, AI can recommend content variations, adapt messaging, and suggest the best distribution channels. This level of personalization enhances the user experience and boosts engagement.

Enhancing Content Strategy with AI-Based Personalization Techniques

Personalization is the key to making your audience feel seen and valued. AI-based personalization techniques take content strategy to the next level.

AI can analyze user data to create user profiles, enabling you to segment your audience effectively. It can then recommend personalized content recommendations, product offerings, or messaging based on individual preferences and behaviors. This not only improves engagement but also increases conversion rates and brand loyalty.

As you embrace AI-driven content creation, it's essential to strike a balance between automation and human creativity. While AI can assist in generating content, your brand's unique voice and authenticity remain crucial. AI should enhance your content strategy, not replace it.

In this chapter, we've uncovered the potential of AI in content creation, from generating text to crafting brand narratives and optimizing content for different channels and audiences. As we continue our exploration, we'll delve into how AI can assist in developing irresistible offers, pricing strategies, and competitive analysis.

THOUGHT STARTERS FOR AI-DRIVEN CONTENT CREATION

1. **Share Your Content Creation Challenges:** Discuss the challenges you face in content creation. How has the volume of content needed for your brand impacted your resources and time?

2. **Explore AI Content Generation Tools:** Research and present AI-powered content generation tools or platforms that have caught your attention. How do they work, and what types of content can they create?

3. **Analyze AI-Generated vs. Human-Created Content**: Compare and contrast AI-generated content with content created by humans. What are the strengths and limitations of each approach?

4. **Craft AI-Generated Brand Messaging:** Use AI content generation tools to create brand messaging or taglines. How well do these AI-generated messages align with your brand's identity?

5. **Enhance Storytelling with AI:** Share examples of brands that have effectively used AI to enhance their storytelling. How did AI contribute to the emotional impact of their narratives?

6. **Discuss the Role of AI in SEO:** Explore how AI can assist in optimizing content for search engines. How does AI-driven SEO impact your brand's visibility and organic reach?

7. **Personalize Content for Different Audiences:** Imagine you have two distinct audience segments. Use AI to generate personalized content for each segment, considering their unique preferences and needs.

8. **Evaluate AI-Generated Content Quality:** Critique AI-generated content for quality and relevance. What criteria do you use to determine if AI-generated

content meets your brand's standards?

9. **Content Consistency Across Channels:** Discuss the importance of maintaining content consistency across various communication channels (website, social media, email, etc.) and how AI can help achieve this.

10. **Explore AI-Enhanced Email Marketing:** Investigate how AI can enhance email marketing campaigns. How can AI-driven personalization and content recommendations improve email engagement?

11. **Ethical Considerations in AI-Generated Content:** Delve into the ethical implications of using AI for content creation. What safeguards should brands have in place to ensure responsible content generation?

12. **The Human Touch in Content Creation:** Share examples of successful content campaigns that have struck a balance between AI-generated and human-created content. How can brands retain their unique voice?

13. **Content Performance Metrics:** Discuss the key metrics and KPIs you track to measure the performance of your AI-generated content. How do these metrics align with your brand's goals?

14. **Content Strategy Adaptation:** Outline a plan for adapting your content strategy to incorporate AI-driven content. How will you integrate AI-generated content seamlessly into your existing strategy?

These thought starters are designed to stimulate discussions, encourage experimentation with AI content generation tools, and promote critical thinking about the role of AI in shaping your brand's content strategy.

10

AI ASSISTANCE CAN PROVE HELPFUL

AI assistance can be valuable across a wide range of channels and areas. Here is a list of various channels where AI assistance can prove helpful.

1. Content Creation and Marketing:

- AI can generate written content, such as blog posts, articles, and product descriptions.

- It can assist in crafting compelling headlines, email subject lines, and social media posts.

- AI-powered tools can optimize content for search engines (SEO).

- Personalized content recommendations can enhance user engagement.

2. Customer Support and Service:

- Chatbots and virtual assistants powered by AI can provide 24/7 customer support.

- AI can assist in automating responses to common customer inquiries.

- Voice recognition and natural language processing (NLP) enable voice-based customer service.

3. Email Marketing:

- AI can personalize email marketing campaigns based on user behavior and preferences.

- Predictive analytics can optimize the timing and content of email communications.

4. E-commerce:

- AI-driven product recommendations enhance the shopping experience.

- Chatbots assist customers in finding products and making purchase decisions.

- AI can optimize pricing strategies and detect fraudulent transactions.

5. Social Media Management:

- AI tools analyze social media trends and sentiment.

- They can schedule posts at optimal times for maximum reach.

- AI can assist in social media ad targeting and optimization.

6. Data Analytics and Insights:

- AI can analyze vast datasets for insights and trends.

- Predictive analytics help in forecasting sales, demand, and market trends.

- AI-driven dashboards and reports provide real-time business insights.

7. Sales and Lead Generation:

- AI can identify potential leads and prioritize them based on likelihood to convert.

- Chatbots can engage with website visitors and capture lead information.

8. Personal Assistants and Productivity:

- Virtual personal assistants like Siri and Alexa use AI for voice recognition and task management.

- AI-powered tools can schedule meetings, set reminders, and automate routine tasks.

9. Finance and Investment:

- AI algorithms analyze financial data for investment recommendations.

- Chatbots can provide financial advice and manage portfolios.

10. Manufacturing and Supply Chain:

- AI optimizes supply chain logistics and demand forecasting.

- Predictive maintenance reduces equipment downtime in manufacturing.

11. Education:

- AI-powered e-learning platforms offer personalized content and recommendations.

- Chatbots assist students with queries and provide immediate feedback.

12. Language Translation:

- AI translation tools offer real-time translation for multilingual communication.

13. Creative Industries:

- AI assists in music composition, artwork generation, and video editing.

- It can analyze user preferences to recommend content in entertainment.

14. Automotive and Transportation:

- Autonomous vehicles use AI for navigation and collision avoidance.

- AI optimizes route planning and traffic management systems.

15. Security and Cybersecurity:

- AI identifies anomalies and potential threats in network traffic.

- Facial recognition and biometric authentication enhance security.

16. Environmental Monitoring:

- AI analyzes data from sensors and satellites to monitor environmental changes.

17. Legal Services:

- AI aids in legal research and contract analysis.

- Chatbots provide legal information and guidance.

18. Government and Public Services:

- AI helps in citizen services, from virtual assistants to data analysis for policy-making.

19. Research and Development:

- AI accelerates scientific research through data analysis and modeling.

AI's remarkable adaptability and versatility render it an invaluable asset across a wide array of industries and communication channels. Its capacity to boost efficiency, aid in informed decision-making, and elevate user experiences is evident. Each passing day unveils fresh applications for the seamless integration of AI. For those who embrace this technology early on, its potential to revolutionize their endeavors cannot be overstated. It has the potential to be a game-changer.

Dive Into the Future of Content Creation!

Dive Into the Future of Content Creation! Discover an extensive collection of AI tools and resources tailored to enhance your creativity. From text generators to image creators, each tool comes with a succinct description and handy links. Perfect for beginners and experts alike, this is your one-stop guide to revolutionizing how you create and innovate. Download now to start exploring and pushing the boundaries of digital content!

standinyourbrandbook.com/generatecontent

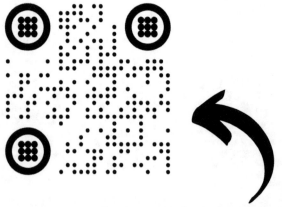

Scan with your phone camera

11

AI-ASSISTED OFFER DEVELOPMENT

In the previous chapters, we've explored how AI can transform various aspects of brand communication, from understanding your audience to creating compelling content. Now, we venture into the realm of offer development, where AI can be a powerful catalyst for creating irresistible products or services that align with your brand's new direction.

Using AI to Identify Product/Service Gaps and Improvements

Offering products or services that resonate with your audience is at the heart of any successful brand. AI can play a pivotal role in this process by helping you identify gaps and opportunities in your current offerings.

Start by analyzing customer feedback and market data. AI algorithms can sift through vast amounts of customer reviews, surveys, and social media discussions to uncover pain points, desires, and unmet needs. This data-driven approach provides valuable insights into where your current offerings excel and where they may fall short.

AI can also assess your competitors' offerings, highlighting areas where your brand can differentiate itself. By identifying gaps in the market and potential improvements to your existing products or services, AI becomes a valuable ally in your quest to create offerings that resonate.

Creating Irresistible Offers That Align with the New Brand Identity

Once you've identified areas for improvement, it's time to craft new offerings that align seamlessly with your brand's new direction. AI can assist in this creative process.

Using predictive analytics, AI can help you forecast demand for potential new products or services. It can also analyze pricing strategies and competitive positioning, ensuring that your offers are not only attractive but also profitable.

Furthermore, AI can generate product or service recommendations based on user behavior and preferences. This personalization enhances the customer experience and increases the likelihood of conversion.

Crafting Winning Proposals

Crafting winning proposals has always been essential in my business journey. It's the key to bridging the gap between my services and my clients' needs. Over time, I've honed this skill, but it wasn't until I embraced AI that I truly felt a game-changing transformation.

AI became more than just a tool; it became my strategic partner in understanding my clients' needs and structuring proposals with exceptional clarity and efficiency. With AI's help, I could decode my clients' challenges and objectives, crafting proposals that felt tailor-made for each one.

But AI wasn't just about content generation. It played a crucial role in determining the right pricing structure, giving me confidence in pricing discussions. As a result, I started winning contracts not only because of competitive pricing but because my proposals demonstrated a deep understanding of my clients' unique needs.

With AI handling the heavy lifting in proposal creation, I had more time for meaningful client interactions, building relationships, and fine-tuning my services. AI became my ally in delivering exceptional value and showcasing my expertise with confidence and precision, leading to success in my business endeavors.

Pricing Strategies and Competitive Analysis with AI Tools

Pricing is a critical component of your brand's offerings. AI can guide your pricing strategy by analyzing market data, competitor pricing, and consumer behavior.

Dynamic pricing, enabled by AI, allows you to adjust prices in real-time based on demand and market conditions. This flexibility can optimize revenue while ensuring your pricing remains competitive.

Competitive analysis tools powered by AI can provide insights into how your competitors are pricing similar products or services. This information helps you position your offerings effectively in the market.

In summary, AI can be a guiding force in the development of irresistible offers that align with your brand's new identity. By identifying gaps, forecasting demand, and optimizing pricing, AI enhances your ability to create offerings that not only attract but also retain your ideal clients.

As we move forward in this book, we'll delve into the practical aspects of rebranding implementation and the role of AI in ensuring brand consistency across all touchpoints.

THOUGHT STARTERS FOR AI-ASSISTED OFFER DEVELOPMENT

1. **Analyze Customer Feedback:** Collect and analyze customer feedback and reviews related to your current offerings. What are the strengths and weaknesses of your existing products or services, as highlighted by customers?

2. **Leverage AI for Competitor Analysis:** Use AI tools to conduct a competitive analysis. What insights can you gather about your competitors' offerings, pricing

strategies, and customer reviews? How can you differentiate your brand?

3. **Identify Unmet Needs:** Explore the potential unmet needs or underserved segments in your market. How can AI-driven market research uncover these opportunities for your brand?

4. **Forecast Demand with AI:** Utilize AI-powered demand forecasting to assess the potential success of new offerings. What factors influence demand, and how can you adjust your strategies accordingly?

5. **Create AI-Generated Product or Service Ideas:** Experiment with AI algorithms to generate ideas for new products or services that align with your brand's values and mission. How can AI assist in the ideation process?

6. **Optimize Pricing with AI:** Discuss the role of AI in pricing strategy. How can dynamic pricing and competitor analysis tools help your brand set competitive and profitable price points?

7. **Personalize Offerings with AI:** Explore how AI can personalize product or service recommendations for individual customers based on their behavior and preferences. How does personalization enhance the customer experience?

8. **Evaluate the Impact of AI on Offer Development:** Reflect on the potential benefits and challenges of integrating AI into the offer development process. How does AI change the way your brand approaches product or service creation?

9. **Case Study Analysis:** Share examples of brands that have successfully used AI to develop and optimize their offerings. What lessons can you draw from their experiences?

10. **Define Key Performance Metrics:** Determine the key performance indicators (KPIs) you will use to measure the success of your AI-assisted offer development. How will you track the impact of these new offerings?

11. **Craft a New Product/Service Pitch:** Using AI-generated insights and ideas, create a pitch or description for a new product or service that aligns with your brand's redefined identity.

12. **Discuss Ethical Considerations:** Explore the ethical implications of using AI in offer development, particularly in areas such as pricing and personalization. How can your brand ensure responsible use of AI in this context?

13. **Plan for Launch and Promotion:** Outline a strategy for launching and promoting your new offerings. How will you communicate their value to your target audience?

These thought starters are designed to encourage discussions, creative brainstorming, and critical thinking about the role of AI in shaping your brand's offers. They can be used as starting points for collaborative exercises and strategic planning within your organization.

12

GENERAL AI-DRIVEN TOOLS FOR RESEARCH

While there are numerous AI-powered platforms available for market research and pricing analysis, not all of them may be specific to your industry. However, you can leverage general AI-driven tools for research and adapt them to your services. Here's a list of free or freemium platforms that can assist in researching service offers and pricing:

1. **Google Trends:** Google Trends provides insights into search query volumes over time. You can use it to identify trending coaching topics and potential demand for specific services.

2. **Google Keyword Planner:** This tool helps you discover relevant keywords related to coaching services. It can provide insights into keyword search volume and competition, helping you refine your offerings.

3. **AnswerThePublic:** This tool generates content ideas by aggregating questions and queries related to specific topics. It can be useful for understanding what

potential coaching clients are curious about.

4. **Facebook Audience Insights:** If you're using Facebook for marketing, Audience Insights can help you understand your target audience's demographics, interests, and behaviors.

5. **LinkedIn Sales Navigator:** For B2B coaching services, LinkedIn's Sales Navigator can help you identify potential clients and their industry-specific needs.

6. **Quora:** Quora is a question-and-answer platform. You can search for service-related questions to understand common concerns and tailor your services accordingly.

7. **SurveyMonkey:** Create surveys to gather feedback and insights from your audience about their coaching needs, willingness to pay, and preferences.

8. **Pricing Tools (e.g., Price2Spy, Prisync):** While some pricing analysis tools have free trials, they offer limited functionality. These tools can help you monitor competitors' pricing strategies.

9. **Google Analytics:** If you have a website, Google Analytics can provide data on user behavior, allowing you to identify popular pages and content.

10. **LinkedIn Insights Tag:** If you have a LinkedIn Marketing Platform account, you can install the Insights Tag to track conversions and gather insights into your website visitors.

11. **OpenAI's GPT-3 Playground:** While not directly for research, you can use GPT-3 to generate responses or content related to your topics, which can aid in content creation and understanding client queries.

12. **Reddit and Subreddits:** Reddit has various subreddits related to business, personal development, and career advice. Monitor discussions to gain insights into common challenges and questions.

13. **AI Chatbots (e.g., ChatGPT):** Implement AI chatbots on your website or social media to engage with potential clients and collect information about their needs.

14. **Ubersuggest:** Ubersuggest provides keyword research, content ideas, and competitive analysis. It can help you understand which topics are in demand.

While these platforms are not tailored exclusively to your industry, they can be adapted to gather insights, identify trends, and understand your potential clients better. Remember to combine these insights with your industry knowledge to refine your service offers and pricing strategies.

13

REBRANDING IMPLEMENTATION STRATEGIES

In the previous chapters, we've laid the foundation for your brand's transformation journey, from understanding your audience to crafting irresistible offers. Now, it's time to bring your rebranding vision to life. In this chapter, we explore the practical strategies and steps for implementing your rebrand effectively.

Planning the Rebranding Process Step-by-Step

Successful rebranding starts with a well-thought-out plan. Begin by defining clear objectives for your rebrand. What specific outcomes are you aiming to achieve? Whether it's expanding your client base, increasing revenue, or enhancing brand perception, setting concrete goals is essential.

Next, create a timeline that outlines the key milestones and deadlines for your rebranding process. This timeline should encompass all aspects, from updating your website and marketing materials to launching new offerings.

Managing Customer Communication During the Transition

During a rebrand, communication is paramount. Your existing clients and audience should be informed about the changes and what they can expect. Transparency builds trust.

Craft a communication strategy that includes:

- **Announcement:** Inform your clients and audience about the rebrand. Explain the reasons behind it and the benefits they can anticipate.

- **Timely Updates:** Keep your audience updated throughout the process. Share milestones, teasers, and sneak peeks.

- **Engagement:** Encourage feedback and engagement. Invite your audience to be part of the journey.

- **Consistency:** Ensure a consistent brand message across all communication channels.

Incorporating AI for Brand Consistency Across All Touchpoints

- Maintaining brand consistency is essential for a successful rebrand. AI can be a valuable tool in this regard. Here's how AI can assist:

- **AI-Powered Design Tools:** AI tools like Adobe Sensei can help you create and update brand visuals consistently.

- **Chatbots and Virtual Assistants:** Implement AI-driven chatbots to ensure consistent messaging and support across your website and social media.

- **Email Marketing Automation:** Use AI to personalize email marketing campaigns, ensuring that your rebrand message reaches each subscriber in a relevant way.

- **Content Management Systems (CMS):** Utilize AI-driven CMS to automate content updates and ensure a unified brand voice across your online presence.

- **Analytics and Monitoring:** AI-driven analytics tools can monitor brand mentions and sentiment across the web, helping you stay on top of your brand's online reputation.

Evaluating the Impact of Your Rebrand

After the rebrand is complete, it's essential to evaluate its impact. Did you achieve your objectives? Are you attracting the clients you aimed for? Are your new offerings resonating with your audience?

AI can play a role here as well. AI-powered analytics can provide insights into changes in customer behavior, website traffic, and conversion rates post-rebrand. This data can inform future decisions and adjustments.

Creating a Long-Term Plan for Continuous Brand Evolution and Growth

Rebranding is not a one-time event; it's an ongoing process. In the fast-paced digital landscape, brands must evolve to remain relevant. Create a long-term plan for continuous brand evolution and growth.

This plan should include regular reviews of your brand's performance, audience feedback, and industry trends. AI-driven market research can be invaluable in identifying new opportunities and threats to your brand.

In summary, rebranding is a journey that requires careful planning, effective communication, and the integration of AI to maintain brand consistency. It's not just about changing your logo or color scheme; it's about aligning your brand with your mission and vision and adapting to meet the ever-changing needs of your clients. In the following chapters, we'll delve into building trust and authority using AI-driven insights and automating brand communication for enhanced efficiency.

THOUGHT STARTERS FOR REBRANDING IMPLEMENTATION STRATEGIES:

1. **Define Your Rebranding Objectives:** Outline the specific objectives and goals you aim to achieve with your rebrand. How will you measure the success of your rebranding efforts?

2. **Create a Rebranding Timeline:** Develop a detailed timeline that includes key milestones and deadlines for each phase of the rebranding process. How will you ensure that your timeline remains on track?

3. **Craft a Communication Strategy:** Describe your communication strategy for announcing and managing the rebrand. How will you ensure transparency and engagement with your audience?

4. **Leverage AI for Visual Brand Consistency:** Explore AI-powered design tools that can assist in maintaining visual brand consistency. How can AI tools help ensure your brand's visual identity is cohesive across all materials?

5. **Implement AI-Driven Chatbots:** Discuss the benefits of using AI-driven chatbots during the rebrand. How can chatbots assist in providing consistent support and messaging during the transition?

6. **Personalize Email Marketing with AI:** Explore how AI can be used to personalize email marketing campaigns during the rebrand. What techniques can be employed to ensure your rebrand message resonates with each subscriber?

7. **Analyze Post-Rebrand Data:** Once the rebrand is complete, analyze post-rebrand data using AI-driven analytics tools. What metrics will you track to evaluate the impact of your rebrand?

8. **Continuous Brand Evolution:** Share your long-term plan for continuous

brand evolution and growth. How will you adapt to changing market dynamics and evolving audience preferences?

9. **Case Study Analysis:** Examine case studies of brands that have successfully implemented rebrands. What strategies and tactics did they employ, and what lessons can you apply to your rebranding efforts?

10. **Ethical Considerations in Rebranding:** Discuss the ethical considerations related to rebranding, such as transparency with customers and maintaining brand authenticity. How will you address these ethical concerns in your rebrand?

11. **Client Feedback and Involvement:** How can you involve your existing clients in the rebranding process? What methods can be used to gather their feedback and ensure their needs are considered?

12. **Brand Monitoring with AI:** Explore AI tools for brand monitoring and sentiment analysis post-rebrand. How can these tools help you stay attuned to your brand's online reputation?

13. **Adapting to Unexpected Challenges:** Rebrands may encounter unexpected challenges. How will you adapt and pivot if unforeseen issues arise during the implementation process?

14. **Creating a Brand Evolution Roadmap:** Develop a roadmap for the ongoing evolution of your brand. How will you stay ahead of industry trends and continuously enhance your brand's offerings?

These thought starters are designed to stimulate discussions, strategic planning, and critical thinking about the practical steps and considerations involved in implementing a successful rebrand. They can be used in workshops, team meetings, or individual reflection as you navigate the rebranding process.

14

BUILDING BRAND TRUST AND AUTHORITY

In the journey of rebranding and reshaping your brand communication, trust and authority are two cornerstones that can elevate your brand to new heights. In this chapter, we'll explore how you can use AI-driven insights and strategies to build trust and establish authority within your industry.

Understanding the Importance of Trust in Brand Success

Trust is the foundation of any successful brand-client relationship. It's the assurance that your brand will consistently deliver on its promises. In the digital age, trust is not just a nice-to-have; it's a necessity.

AI can play a crucial role in understanding and fostering trust. Through sentiment analysis and feedback aggregation, AI tools can provide real-time insights into how your audience perceives your brand. These insights can help you identify areas where trust may be eroding and take proactive measures to address them.

Leveraging AI-Generated Social Proof and Testimonials

Social proof is a potent tool for building trust. When potential clients see others endorsing your brand, they are more likely to trust your offerings.

AI can help you gather and showcase social proof effectively. AI-driven tools can analyze customer reviews, social media mentions, and testimonials to identify the most impactful endorsements. These tools can also automate the process of displaying these endorsements on your website and marketing materials.

The Impact of Feedback and Testimonials

After the initial launch of my Brand Accelerator Course, I recognized the importance of gathering feedback and testimonials to improve and attract more clients for the next offering. Through surveys and interviews, I learned about the challenges my clients faced and what aspects of the course needed enhancement. The real gems were the testimonials, showcasing the genuine impact the course had on participants' brand communication.

Armed with this valuable feedback and compelling testimonials, I revamped the course for its second run. I tailored the content to address specific client challenges, created additional resources, and made practical improvements. I prominently featured these testimonials to demonstrate the course's value to potential clients.

The results were impressive. The second offering attracted more participants who reported even higher satisfaction levels. This experience underscored the importance of listening, gathering information, and using feedback to enhance my offerings. It's an ongoing process that continues to help me refine my courses and attract clients genuinely excited about transforming their brand communication.

Nurturing Brand Authority Through Thought Leadership and AI-Driven Insights

Authority in your industry positions your brand as a trusted source of expertise. It's a powerful way to attract clients who seek guidance and solutions.

AI can enhance your authority-building efforts by providing data-driven insights. AI tools can analyze industry trends, competitor strategies, and customer behavior to identify opportunities for thought leadership. By sharing data-backed insights, your brand can become a recognized authority in your niche.

Personalized Recommendations and AI-Driven Content

Trust and authority are also built through personalization. When your brand understands individual client needs and preferences, it can offer tailored solutions.

AI-driven personalization extends to content recommendations and product or service suggestions. By analyzing user behavior and historical data, AI can recommend content and offerings that align with each client's unique interests. This level of personalization enhances the client experience and reinforces trust.

The Role of AI in Client Engagement and Feedback Analysis

Engaging with your clients and gathering feedback is essential for maintaining trust. AI-powered chatbots and virtual assistants can provide immediate support and engagement on your website and social media.

AI can also assist in analyzing client feedback. Natural language processing (NLP) algorithms can extract valuable insights from client reviews and comments, helping you address concerns and continually improve your offerings, content, and marketing.

In summary, building trust and authority is an ongoing process that requires data-driven insights, effective social proof, and personalized engagement. AI provides the tools and capabilities to strengthen these aspects of your brand communication. As we continue our journey, we'll explore the automation of brand communication through AI-powered chatbots and virtual assistants in Chapter 8.

THOUGHT STARTERS FOR BUILDING BRAND TRUST & AUTHORITY

1. **Define Brand Trust:** In your own words, what does "brand trust" mean, and why is it important in the context of your brand and industry?

2. **Assessing Trust Perception:** How do you currently perceive the level of trust your audience has in your brand? Are there specific areas where trust may need improvement?

3. **The Impact of Trust on Brand Loyalty:** Discuss the relationship between trust and brand loyalty. How does trust influence client retention and advocacy?

4. **AI-Generated Social Proof:** Share examples of brands that effectively use AI to showcase social proof. How can AI-driven testimonials and endorsements enhance trust in your brand?

5. **Building Trust Through Transparency:** How can your brand use AI-driven transparency to build trust? What specific aspects of your operations can be made more transparent?

6. **Thought Leadership Strategies:** Explore thought leadership strategies that can establish your brand's authority in your industry. How can AI-driven insights support these strategies?

7. **Case Study Analysis:** Examine case studies of brands that have successfully built trust and authority in their respective industries. What strategies did they employ, and how can you adapt them to your brand?

8. **AI in Content Personalization:** Discuss the role of AI in personalizing content and recommendations for clients. How can personalization enhance trust

and engagement?

9. **Client Engagement Through AI:** Share ideas on how AI-driven chatbots and virtual assistants can engage with clients effectively. How can AI-powered engagement tools strengthen trust-building efforts?

10. **Managing Negative Feedback:** How should your brand handle negative feedback and criticism? Discuss AI-driven strategies for addressing and learning from client concerns.

11. **Measuring Brand Authority:** How can your brand measure its authority within the industry? What key metrics and indicators can AI assist in tracking?

12. **Leveraging AI Insights:** Share examples of how AI-driven insights have influenced your brand's decision-making processes. How can these insights enhance your authority in your niche?

13. **The Role of AI in Building Trust with Data:** Explore the ethical considerations of using AI for data analysis and personalization. How can your brand ensure responsible use of client data in trust-building efforts?

14. **Client Testimonials and Stories:** Encourage clients to share their success stories and testimonials. How can these narratives contribute to building trust and authority for your brand?

These thought starters are designed to facilitate discussions, reflections, and strategic planning to enhance your brand's trustworthiness and authority. They can be used in team meetings, workshops, or as self-assessment exercises to refine your brand communication strategies.

15

TURNING TO AI TO ENHANCE MARKETING STRATEGIES

Influencers and coaches are increasingly turning to AI to enhance their marketing strategies, using technology to gain deeper insights into their audiences, personalize content, and streamline their operations. Here's how some famous experts could use AI for these applications.

Audience Analysis and Personalization:

- **Amy Porterfield** and **Neil Patel** can use AI for audience analysis. AI tools can track user interactions, preferences, and behaviors, providing valuable data that can be used to tailor marketing messages and offerings. For instance, Neil Patel's Ubersuggest uses AI to understand SEO trends, which helps users optimize their websites and content strategies.

- **Marie Forleo** could leverage AI to segment her audience and personalize communications. This helps in delivering targeted content that resonates with specific audience segments, increasing engagement and conversion rates.

Content Optimization and Strategy:

- **Jay Shetty** could be utilizing AI for analyzing content performance on social media. AI tools can identify which types of content are most engaging, helping influencers like Jay tailor their future content to audience preferences.

- **Tim Ferriss** could use AI to optimize his blog and podcast content. By understanding what topics and formats are most appealing to his audience, he can strategically plan his content to maximize reach and impact.

Efficiency in Operations and Time Management:

- **Simon Sinek** and **Rachel Botsman** could use AI to streamline their operational tasks. AI can automate routine tasks like scheduling, email responses, and data analysis, allowing them more time to focus on content creation and audience engagement.

- **Seth Godin** and **Vanessa Van Edwards** might employ AI for market analysis and customer behavior predictions, making their marketing efforts more efficient and targeted.

Research and Development of New Insights:

- **Brené Brown** could use AI to analyze large volumes of qualitative data. For influencers and coaches, this approach can lead to new insights into human behavior and preferences, enhancing the depth and relevance of their content.

Enhanced Storytelling and Engagement:

- AI can also assist in crafting narratives that are more likely to resonate with audiences. For example, **Mel Robbins** could use AI to analyze speech patterns or audience responses, helping her craft more engaging and impactful motivational speeches.

In summary, influencers and coaches are using AI to gain a more nuanced understanding of their audiences, create more personalized and effective content, streamline their operations, develop new insights, and enhance their storytelling and engagement techniques. This strategic use of AI not only helps in building their personal brands but also ensures that they can deliver more value to their followers and clients.

16

AUTOMATING BRAND COMMUNICATION

In the rapidly changing landscape of brand communication, automation has emerged as a transformative tool that not only saves time but also enhances the client experience. This chapter delves into the ways in which AI-powered chatbots and virtual assistants can streamline your brand's interactions, freeing up valuable resources for more strategic tasks.

Integrating AI-Powered Chatbots and Virtual Assistants

The integration of AI-powered chatbots and virtual assistants is a pivotal step in enhancing your brand's communication. These intelligent tools serve as the front-line ambassadors of your brand, available round the clock to engage with clients. They possess the capability to handle a wide range of tasks, from answering frequently asked questions to guiding clients through your product or service offerings.

One of the primary advantages of these AI-driven entities is their ability to provide instant responses, ensuring that clients receive timely assistance. This not only leads to improved client satisfaction but also allows your team to focus on more complex and strategic aspects of brand management. By automating routine interactions, you can deliver consistent and efficient support, reinforcing your brand's commitment to clarity and professionalism.

Streamlining Customer Interactions and Support

AI-powered chatbots are invaluable in streamlining customer interactions and providing efficient support. They can effortlessly manage routine inquiries, such as order status, account information, and basic troubleshooting. By automating these repetitive tasks, your team can dedicate more time to addressing unique client needs and complex issues.

Moreover, chatbots offer a personalized experience by analyzing client data and tailoring responses accordingly. They can recommend relevant products or services based on the client's history and preferences, thereby increasing the likelihood of cross-selling or upselling. This personalized approach not only enhances the client experience but also contributes to the brand's reputation for providing solutions with confidence and precision.

Implementing AI for Personalized Email Marketing Campaigns

Email marketing remains a potent tool for client engagement, and AI has revolutionized this aspect of brand communication. AI-driven email marketing tools excel in analyzing client behavior, past interactions, and preferences. With this data-driven insight, you can craft highly personalized email campaigns that resonate with each individual recipient.

Personalization goes beyond simply addressing clients by their first name. AI can dynamically adjust email content to include product recommendations, relevant content, and exclusive offers that align with the client's interests and purchase history. This level of customization not only increases open and click-through rates but also drives conversions, as clients feel that the brand genuinely understands their needs and desires.

By leveraging AI in email marketing, your brand demonstrates a deep commitment to connecting with clients on a personal level. This aligns seamlessly with the core values of clarity, confidence, and compassion, as clients receive content that is not only informative but also highly relevant to their unique preferences.

Enhancing Efficiency in Client Communication

Efficiency in client communication is crucial for building trust and satisfaction. AI-driven virtual assistants excel in enhancing efficiency by automating various administrative tasks. These virtual assistants can manage your calendar, schedule appointments, and send reminders, ensuring that client interactions are organized and timely.

For instance, imagine a scenario where a potential client expresses interest in your services through your website. An AI-powered virtual assistant can instantly schedule a consultation, eliminating the need for back-and-forth emails or phone calls. This swift and efficient response not only impresses the client but also reflects positively on your brand's commitment to delivering a seamless client experience.

Additionally, virtual assistants can automate follow-up emails and appointment confirmations, reducing the likelihood of missed meetings and enhancing overall client satisfaction. Clients appreciate brands that respect their time and provide efficient communication, which further reinforces trust and loyalty.

AI-Driven Insights for Improved Communication

AI is not only a facilitator of communication but also a valuable source of insights for brand improvement. AI tools can analyze client interactions, feedback, and communication patterns to provide data-driven insights that inform decision-making.

By mining chatbot interactions, for example, you can identify common client queries, concerns, and challenges. Armed with this information, your brand can proactively address these issues, improving the client experience and demonstrating your commitment to compassionate problem-solving.

AI-driven sentiment analysis can also gauge client satisfaction and sentiment trends. Identifying trends in client sentiment allows your brand to make data-backed adjustments to communication strategies and offerings, ultimately strengthening client trust.

Balancing Automation with a Human Touch

While AI automation offers numerous benefits, it's crucial to strike a balance between automation and the human touch. Clients value authentic interactions with humans, especially in situations that require empathy and understanding.

AI should complement, not replace, these human interactions. When a client faces a complex issue or seeks emotional support, it's essential to seamlessly transition to a human agent who can provide the necessary care and compassion.

The balance between automation and the human touch reinforces the brand's commitment to both efficiency and empathy, aligning with the values of clarity, confidence, and compassion.

Ensuring Data Privacy and Ethical AI Use

As you implement AI in client communication, it's paramount to prioritize data privacy and ethical AI use. Clients must trust that their information is handled responsibly and that AI-driven interactions are conducted with integrity.

Robust data protection measures should be in place to safeguard client data, including encryption, access controls, and compliance with data protection regulations such as GDPR or CCPA. Regular audits of AI systems ensure that they adhere to ethical guidelines and avoid biases or discriminatory practices.

By prioritizing data privacy and ethical AI use, your brand not only builds trust but also sets a standard for responsible AI implementation in the industry.

Continuous Learning and Adaptation

AI is not a static tool; it continually evolves. Staying updated with the latest advancements in AI-driven communication tools is essential to maintaining your brand's competitive edge and ensuring that client communication remains efficient and effective.

Regularly seek feedback from clients regarding their interactions with AI-driven tools. This feedback can provide valuable insights into areas for improvement and customization. Continuously adapting and refining your AI communication strategies ensures that your brand remains at the forefront of innovative client engagement.

In summary, the integration of AI-powered chatbots and virtual assistants into your brand communication streamlines processes, enhances efficiency, and allows your team to focus on high-value interactions. These tools align with your brand's values of clarity, confidence, and compassion, as they provide efficient and meaningful communication experiences for your clients. As we move forward, we'll delve into the role of AI in data analytics and decision-making in Chapter 9, where we'll explore how AI can provide real-time insights to drive brand growth.

THOUGHT STARTERS FOR AUTOMATING BRAND COMMUNICATION

1. **Benefits of AI-Powered Chatbots:** Discuss the advantages of integrating AI-powered chatbots into your brand communication. How can they enhance client interactions and streamline processes?

2. **Improving Client Support:** Share examples of how AI-driven chatbots can improve client support by handling routine inquiries. How can these tools ensure consistent and efficient support?

3. **Personalized Email Marketing:** Explore the concept of personalized email marketing campaigns driven by AI. How can personalized emails strengthen client engagement and drive conversions?

4. **Efficiency in Client Communication:** How can AI-powered virtual assistants enhance the efficiency of your client communication? Discuss specific tasks that virtual assistants can manage to improve brand-client interactions.

5. **AI-Driven Insights:** Share instances where AI has provided valuable insights into client communication patterns. How can these insights inform your brand's messaging and strategy?

6. **Balancing Automation and the Human Touch:** Discuss the importance of maintaining a balance between AI-driven automation and human interactions. When is it appropriate to use AI, and when should human intervention be prioritized?

7. **Data Privacy and Ethical AI:** Explore the ethical considerations of using AI in client communication. How can your brand ensure data privacy and responsible AI use in interactions?

8. **Client Feedback on Automation:** Gather feedback from clients about their experiences with AI-powered communication tools. How have clients responded to automation, and what improvements can be made?

9. **AI in Client Appointment Scheduling:** Share examples of AI-powered appointment scheduling systems. How can such tools enhance the client experience and brand efficiency?

10. **Continuous Learning and Adaptation:** Discuss the need for ongoing learning and adaptation when integrating AI into brand communication. How can your brand stay updated with the latest AI advancements in this context?

11. **Case Studies of Successful AI Integration:** Examine case studies of brands that have successfully integrated AI into their communication strategies. What lessons can you draw from their experiences?

12. **Exploring Chatbot Platforms:** Research and discuss different chatbot platforms and tools available for your brand. What features and capabilities do they offer, and how do they align with your communication goals?

13. **Automation ROI:** Evaluate the return on investment (ROI) of implementing AI-driven automation in brand communication. How can you measure the impact of automation on efficiency and client satisfaction?

14. **AI-Enhanced Client Engagement:** Share ideas on how AI can enhance client engagement beyond traditional support. How can AI-driven tools provide value-added experiences to clients?

These thought starters are designed to facilitate discussions, explorations, and reflections on the role of AI in automating brand communication. They can be used in team meetings, workshops, or individual reflections as you consider the practical implications of integrating AI into your communication strategies.

17

AI-POWERED CHATBOT AND VIRTUAL ASSISTANT PLATFORMS

1. **Dialogflow by Google:** Offers natural language processing and understanding for building chatbots and voice applications.

2. **IBM Watson Assistant:** Enables businesses to build and deploy conversational interfaces into any application, device, or channel.

3. **Amazon Lex:** Amazon's AI service for building conversational interfaces into applications using voice and text.

4. **Microsoft Bot Framework:** A comprehensive platform for building, connecting, and deploying chatbots across various channels.

5. **Chatfuel:** A no-code platform for creating AI chatbots for Facebook Messenger

and other messaging platforms.

6. **ManyChat:** Focused on Facebook Messenger, it helps create AI chatbots for marketing and customer support.

7. **Zoho Desk:** Offers AI-powered chatbots for customer service and support.

8. **Tars:** A platform for building conversational landing pages, chatbots, and virtual assistants.

9. **Intercom:** Combines chatbots with live chat for customer engagement and support.

10. **HubSpot Chatbot Builder:** Part of the HubSpot CRM, it helps create chatbots for lead generation and customer interactions.

11. **Pandorabots:** Offers a chatbot development platform with AI and machine learning capabilities.

12. **Rasa:** An open-source platform for building conversational AI chatbots with a focus on customization.

13. **Wit.ai by Facebook:** Allows developers to build natural language understanding into applications, bots, and IoT devices.

14. **Bold360 by LogMeIn:** Offers AI-powered chatbots and virtual assistants for customer engagement and support.

15. **Kore.ai:** Provides AI-powered chatbots and virtual assistants for customer service, HR, and IT support.

16. **Ada Support:** Offers AI-powered chatbots for automating customer support and improving user experience.

17. **Inbenta:** Provides AI chatbots and virtual assistants for e-commerce, customer support, and knowledge management.

18. **Gupshup:** Offers chatbot development and messaging platform for businesses.

19. **Turing.com:** Connects businesses with remote software developers specializing

in AI chatbot development.

20. **SAP Conversational AI:** Enables the creation of AI chatbots for automating tasks and interactions.

21. **Aivo:** Offers AI-powered virtual assistants for customer support and engagement.

22. **Kuki Chatbot:** Provides AI-driven chatbots for e-commerce, customer support, and lead generation.

23. **Rulai:** Focuses on AI-powered chatbots for enterprise customer service and automation.

24. **Flow XO:** A platform for building chatbots and automating workflows with AI.

25. **Verloop:** Offers AI-driven chatbots and customer support automation for businesses.

These platforms vary in terms of features, capabilities, and pricing, so it's essential to evaluate them based on your specific business needs and use cases.

18

AI IN DATA ANALYTICS AND DECISION MAKING

In today's data-driven landscape, the ability to derive real-time insights from vast datasets is a competitive advantage. AI tools excel in processing and analyzing data at speeds and scales that human capabilities cannot match. By harnessing the power of AI-driven data analysis, your brand gains a significant edge in understanding client behavior, market trends, and the overall health of your business.

AI-driven data analysis involves parsing through structured and unstructured data sources, such as website interactions, social media mentions, and customer reviews, to extract meaningful patterns and trends. It enables your brand to track client sentiments, monitor emerging market shifts, and identify areas for improvement or innovation. This invaluable information forms the foundation of informed decision-making, allowing your brand to adapt swiftly to changing dynamics, optimize strategies, and enhance client experiences.

Making Data-Driven Decisions for Brand Growth

Collecting data is just the beginning; the true power lies in leveraging that data to drive brand growth. AI facilitates data-driven decision-making by providing actionable insights that align with your brand's mission and vision. By analyzing historical and real-time data, AI can help your brand identify growth opportunities, streamline processes, and optimize resource allocation.

For instance, AI can identify previously unnoticed client segments with untapped potential, allowing your brand to tailor offerings and marketing strategies accordingly. It can also forecast demand trends, enabling you to proactively address client needs. Data-driven decisions foster a culture of adaptability and continuous improvement within your brand, ensuring that strategies remain aligned with evolving market dynamics and client preferences.

Understanding AI-Generated Analytics Reports

AI-generated analytics reports serve as a treasure trove of information about your brand's performance. These reports encompass a wide range of metrics, including website traffic, conversion rates, client demographics, and more. Understanding how to interpret these reports is essential for harnessing the insights they provide.

AI-powered analytics reports not only offer retrospective data but can also provide predictive and prescriptive insights. They help your brand understand the impact of past decisions, make informed choices for the future, and evaluate the effectiveness of ongoing strategies. A thorough grasp of these reports empowers your team to extract actionable insights and steer your brand towards sustained growth.

Predictive Analytics and Forecasting with AI

Predictive analytics, a hallmark of AI, offers the ability to forecast future trends and outcomes based on historical data. This capability is a game-changer for your brand, as it allows you to anticipate client needs and stay ahead of the competition.

By analyzing past client behaviors, market dynamics, and external factors, AI can generate predictive models that project future trends. For example, it can forecast which products or services are likely to gain traction, enabling your brand to proactively meet client demands. This proactive approach not only enhances client satisfaction but also positions your brand as an industry leader capable of anticipating market shifts.

Implementing AI-Driven Marketing Campaigns

AI is a powerful ally in optimizing marketing campaigns. It excels at analyzing client behavior and preferences, enabling your brand to tailor marketing efforts to specific segments and individuals. This personalization significantly enhances the effectiveness of your outreach.

AI-driven marketing encompasses various aspects, including personalized content recommendations, dynamic pricing strategies, and targeted advertising. For instance, AI can analyze a client's browsing history and purchase behavior to suggest products or services that align with their interests. It can also optimize ad placements and budgets to maximize ROI. The result is a more engaging and relevant client experience, leading to higher conversion rates and brand loyalty.

Real-Time Feedback Loops and Iterative Decision-Making

One of AI's most valuable contributions to decision-making is its ability to facilitate real-time feedback loops. These loops enable your brand to adjust strategies and tactics promptly based on emerging data and insights. This iterative decision-making process ensures that your brand remains agile and responsive to changing market dynamics.

AI-driven feedback loops are particularly beneficial in highly competitive industries or during periods of rapid change. For example, if a marketing campaign is not delivering the expected results, AI can quickly identify underperforming elements and recommend adjustments. This real-time adaptability allows your brand to make data-backed decisions that maximize efficiency and effectiveness.

AI-Enhanced Risk Management

Effective risk management is essential for brand sustainability. AI's analytical prowess extends to risk assessment by analyzing market data, client feedback, and external factors. This comprehensive analysis enables your brand to identify potential risks proactively and develop mitigation strategies.

AI can help your brand assess risks in various areas, such as market volatility, cybersecurity threats, or supply chain disruptions. By monitoring and analyzing relevant data sources, AI can provide early warnings and insights that empower your brand to take preemptive actions. Effective risk management not only safeguards your brand's reputation but also ensures business continuity and client trust.

The Ethical Use of AI in Decision-Making

While AI offers immense potential for data analytics, it's paramount to consider the ethical implications of its use. Responsible and ethical AI usage involves considerations related to data privacy, fairness, and transparency. Your brand must uphold ethical standards in decision-making processes to maintain client trust and societal integrity.

Ethical AI use encompasses various principles, including:

1. **Data Privacy:** Ensuring that client data is handled with the utmost care, following industry standards and legal regulations.

2. **Bias Mitigation**: Implementing measures to identify and mitigate biases in AI algorithms to ensure fair treatment of all clients.

3. **Transparency:** Providing transparency in AI-driven decisions by explaining the rationale and factors behind automated recommendations.

4. **Accountability:** Establishing clear lines of responsibility for AI-driven decisions and outcomes within your brand.

5. **Consent and Control:** Allowing clients to have control over their data and the extent to which AI influences their experiences.

Your brand's commitment to ethical AI use not only strengthens client trust but also contributes to a positive brand image.

Building a Data-Driven Culture

To fully capitalize on AI-driven data analytics, your brand should foster a data-driven culture. This cultural shift involves training your team to interpret data effectively, utilize AI tools, and embrace a mindset that values data-driven insights as integral to decision-making.

Creating a data-driven culture begins with education and training programs that empower your team members with the necessary skills to work with data and AI tools. Team members should understand how to extract actionable insights from data, interpret AI-generated reports, and apply these insights to their roles effectively.

Encourage a mindset of curiosity and continuous improvement, where team members actively seek opportunities to leverage data-driven insights in their decision-making processes. Recognize and reward individuals and teams for their data-driven achievements, fostering a culture that values and celebrates data-informed choices.

Case Studies of Data-Driven Success

To gain a deeper understanding of the potential impact of AI-driven data analytics, explore case studies of brands that have successfully harnessed AI to inform decision-making and drive growth. These case studies offer real-world examples of strategies and tools employed by brands across diverse industries.

Analyze the strategies and approaches that these brands took to leverage AI for data-driven decision-making. Consider how their experiences and successes can be applied to your brand's context, ensuring that you derive maximum value from AI-driven insights.

Creating an AI-Enhanced Decision-Making Framework

As you embark on the journey of integrating AI into your brand's decision-making processes, it's essential to develop a comprehensive framework that defines how AI-generated insights will be incorporated into strategic planning, marketing, client engagement, and other areas of your brand.

This framework should outline the following:

1. **Data Sources:** Identify the sources of data that will be collected and analyzed by AI, ensuring that they align with your brand's objectives and ethical standards.

2. **Analysis Methods:** Specify the AI algorithms and tools that will be used for data analysis, considering their suitability for different types of data.

3. **Decision Integration:** Determine how AI-generated insights will be integrated into decision-making processes. Define roles and responsibilities for deci-

sion-makers and AI systems.

4. **Feedback and Continuous Improvement:** Establish mechanisms for gathering feedback on AI-driven decisions and iterate on strategies based on feedback and evolving data.

5. **Ethical Guidelines:** Document ethical guidelines and principles that govern AI usage within your brand, emphasizing data privacy, fairness, and transparency.

6. **Training and Education:** Describe the training and education programs that will equip your team members with the necessary skills and knowledge to work effectively with AI and data.

By creating a structured framework, your brand ensures that AI-driven insights are seamlessly integrated into decision-making processes, enhancing efficiency, effectiveness, and adaptability.

In conclusion, AI has the potential to revolutionize how your brand collects, analyzes, and acts on data. By embracing AI-driven data analytics, you can make more informed decisions, seize opportunities, and navigate challenges effectively. The journey of harnessing AI continues in Chapter 10, where we explore how AI can help your brand regain time freedom by automating time-consuming tasks, allowing you to focus on strategic initiatives and client relationships.

THOUGHT STARTERS FOR UNDERSTANDING AI IN DATA ANALYTICS AND DECISION MAKING

1. **The Role of Data in Brand Decision-Making:** Discuss the importance of data in informing brand decisions. How can data-driven decisions lead to brand growth?

2. **AI Tools for Data Analysis:** Explore AI tools and technologies used for data analysis. How can these tools assist in processing and interpreting large datasets?

3. **Case Studies of Data-Driven Success:** Analyze case studies of brands that have achieved success through data-driven decision-making. What specific strategies and insights led to their growth?

4. **Understanding AI-Generated Analytics Reports:** Describe your understanding of AI-generated analytics reports. What types of data and metrics should your brand monitor regularly?

5. **Using Predictive Analytics:** Discuss the concept of predictive analytics. How can AI-driven predictive models help your brand anticipate future trends and client behavior?

6. **Implementing Real-Time Feedback Loops:** Share ideas on how your brand can implement real-time feedback loops using AI. How can these loops enhance decision-making and agility?

7. **Ethical Considerations in AI Data Analysis:** Explore the ethical considerations related to AI in data analysis. How can your brand ensure responsible and ethical use of client data?

8. **Data-Driven Marketing Campaigns:** Discuss the benefits of AI-driven marketing campaigns. How can AI personalize marketing efforts to improve engagement and conversions?

9. **Building a Data-Driven Culture:** What steps can your brand take to foster a data-driven culture within your team? How can you encourage data literacy and utilization?

10. **Risk Management with AI:** How can AI assist in identifying and mitigating risks to your brand? Discuss specific risk scenarios and how AI can provide insights.

11. **Interpreting AI Insights:** Share experiences or challenges related to interpreting AI-generated insights. How can your brand ensure that these insights are translated into actionable strategies?

12. **AI and Innovation:** How can AI-driven data analytics support innovation within your brand? Discuss ways in which data insights can lead to innovative product or service offerings.

13. **Feedback and Iteration:** Describe your brand's approach to collecting client feedback and using it for iterative decision-making. How can AI assist in this process?

14. **Creating a Decision-Making Framework**: Develop a framework for integrating AI-generated insights into your brand's decision-making processes. How will data analytics influence strategic planning and execution?

These thought starters are designed to stimulate discussions, reflections, and strategic planning related to the use of AI in data analytics and decision-making. They can be used in team meetings, workshops, or individual reflections as you explore the transformative potential of AI in your brand's decision-making processes.

19

SOURCES FOR GATHERING DATA ANALYTICS

In today's data-driven world, small businesses have a variety of sources to gather analytics, each offering unique insights and opportunities for growth. From understanding customer behavior to optimizing operations, these data sources are vital in making informed decisions and staying competitive. Below are some key places where small businesses can collect valuable data analytics:

1. **Website Analytics Tools:**

- Google Analytics: Provides insights into website traffic, user behavior, and conversion rates.

- Adobe Analytics: Offers detailed web analytics and real-time data.

2. **Social Media Analytics:**

- Facebook Insights: Provides data on engagement, reach, and demographics for your Facebook Page.

- Twitter Analytics: Offers insights into your Twitter account's performance and audience.

3. **Email Marketing Platforms:**

- Awebber: Offers email campaign analytics, including open rates, click-through rates, and subscriber behavior.

- Constant Contact: Provides email marketing analytics and reporting tools.

4. **E-commerce Platforms:**

- Shopify Analytics: Offers data on sales, customer behavior, and product performance for e-commerce businesses.

- WooCommerce Analytics: Provides insights for WordPress-based online stores.

5. **Customer Relationship Management (CRM) Software:**

- Salesforce: Offers analytics and reporting features to track sales, customer interactions, and leads.

- HubSpot CRM: Provides analytics on marketing, sales, and customer service activities.

6. **Point-of-Sale (POS) Systems:**

- Square Analytics: Offers sales and inventory data for businesses using Square's POS system.

- Lightspeed Analytics: Provides retail and restaurant analytics for businesses using Lightspeed POS.

7. **Financial Software:**

- QuickBooks: Offers financial analytics and reporting for small businesses.

- Xero: Provides financial data and insights for accounting purposes.

8. Survey and Feedback Tools:

 - SurveyMonkey: Allows businesses to create surveys and gather data on customer opinions and preferences.

- Typeform: Offers customizable surveys and forms for gathering feedback.

9. Online Advertising Platforms:

- Google Ads: Provides analytics on the performance of online advertising campaigns.

 - Facebook Ads Manager: Offers insights into the effectiveness of Facebook and Instagram ads.

10. Local SEO Tools:

- Moz Local: Provides analytics and insights for local search engine optimization efforts.

- BrightLocal: Offers local SEO reporting and analytics for small businesses.

11. Market Research and Industry Reports:

- Statista: Offers access to a wide range of statistical data and industry reports.

- IBISWorld: Provides industry-specific market research reports.

12. Government Data Sources:

 - U.S. Small Business Administration (SBA): Offers data and resources for small businesses in the United States.

- Census Bureau Data: Provides demographic and economic data that can be useful for market analysis.

13. Online Surveys and Questionnaires:

- Google Forms: Allows businesses to create custom surveys and questionnaires to gather data from customers or employees.

- SurveyGizmo: Offers survey creation and data analysis tools.

14. **Customer Reviews and Feedback Platforms:**

 - Yelp: Provides insights into customer reviews and ratings for businesses in various industries.

 - Trustpilot: Offers a platform for collecting and displaying customer reviews and feedback.

15. **Web Scraping Tools and Services:**

- Import.io: Allows businesses to extract data from websites for competitive analysis and market research.

- WebHarvy: Offers web scraping software for gathering data from websites.

16. **Trade Associations and Industry Publications:**

 - Explore trade associations and industry-specific publications that often provide valuable data and insights related to your business niche.

Remember to use these data sources responsibly and ensure compliance with data privacy regulations, especially when dealing with customer data. Data analytics can help small businesses make informed decisions, improve operations, and better understand their customers and markets.

20

REGAINING TIME FREEDOM WITH AI AUTOMATION

In the journey to optimize your brand communication, one of the most precious assets you can gain is time. Time is the foundation upon which you can build deeper client relationships, refine your offerings, and enhance your brand's impact. In this chapter, we explore how AI automation can help you reclaim this invaluable resource.

Reclaiming Time with the Help of AI

I once worked with a client who was passionate about her brand but struggled with limited time for critical tasks like refining her target audience, creating a new offering, and revamping her brand communication. Typically, these tasks would take her one to two weeks due to interruptions in her daily schedule.

To expedite her brand transformation, we turned to ChatGPT, an AI-powered platform, for market research and content generation. In a focused session, Chat-

GPT provided insights into her ideal audience and emerging market trends within minutes.

The most remarkable part was the swift content creation. With ChatGPT's assistance, we generated clear, emotionally resonant brand messaging tailored to different channels and audiences. What would have taken weeks was accomplished in a fraction of the time.

The client was thrilled with the newfound clarity and her exciting new offer. With ChatGPT, she streamlined her brand transformation and regained precious time for connecting with clients and pursuing her passion.

This story illustrates how AI, specifically ChatGPT, can significantly enhance brand communication by saving time and enhancing clarity. It shows that with the right tools and innovation, we can achieve our goals more efficiently and focus on what matters most.

Identifying Time-Consuming Tasks

In the pursuit of optimizing brand communication, recognizing and addressing time-consuming tasks is the first step towards regaining time freedom. As the founder of a small business, I am well aware of the importance of efficient communication. However, daily responsibilities often include repetitive and resource-draining activities that divert your attention from strategic endeavors. Identifying these tasks is crucial for effective time management.

Begin by conducting a comprehensive review of your daily and weekly routines. Pay close attention to tasks that are repetitive, manual, or involve extensive administrative work. Common examples include data entry, email management, social media monitoring, and scheduling appointments. By pinpointing these time-intensive activities, you can strategize their automation and free up valuable time for more impactful endeavors.

AI-Based Project Management and Scheduling Tools

AI-powered project management and scheduling tools offer a transformative solution to reclaim time. These sophisticated systems can automate task allocation, set reminders, and optimize project timelines. By integrating AI into your project management, you gain greater control over your schedule and reduce the cognitive load associated with juggling multiple projects simultaneously.

AI-driven tools can efficiently handle project coordination, ensuring that deadlines are met, resources are allocated effectively, and team members are informed of their responsibilities. This automation not only streamlines project management but also enhances your ability to focus on high-priority tasks, such as client engagement and strategy development.

Delegating Routine Brand Management Tasks to AI Systems

Routine brand management tasks can consume a significant portion of your time. These tasks often include monitoring social media engagement, responding to common client inquiries, and managing email communications. AI systems excel in handling these routine responsibilities, offering both time savings and consistent client interactions.

AI-driven chatbots and virtual assistants can engage with clients in real-time, providing immediate responses to frequently asked questions. They can also categorize and prioritize client inquiries, ensuring that urgent matters are addressed promptly. This automation not only enhances client satisfaction but also allows you to redirect your attention to strategic aspects of brand communication.

AI-Enhanced Content Creation and Publishing

Content creation is a cornerstone of effective brand communication, but it can be a labor-intensive process. AI-powered content generation tools can be invaluable in expediting content creation and publication. These tools can assist in drafting blog posts, generating social media updates, and even crafting email newsletters.

AI algorithms can analyze trending topics, client preferences, and industry insights to suggest relevant content ideas. They can also automate the generation of content based on predefined templates and guidelines. By harnessing AI for content creation, you can maintain a consistent publishing schedule, engage your audience with fresh content, and allocate your creative energies to more strategic endeavors.

Client Engagement at Scale

Maintaining meaningful client engagement, especially during high-demand periods, is a challenge that AI-driven chatbots and virtual assistants are well-equipped to address. These automated systems can engage with clients at scale, providing support, answering inquiries, and offering personalized recommendations.

AI chatbots can serve as the first point of contact for clients, assisting with common queries and directing clients to relevant resources. They can also initiate proactive engagement by sending personalized messages, product recommendations, or event invitations based on client behavior and preferences. This automation ensures that every client feels valued and attended to, even as your client base grows.

The Human Element in Chatbot Automations

The human element plays a pivotal role in the creation of chatbot automations, complementing AI's efficiency with empathy, understanding, complex problem-solving, and ethical decision-making. Human agents excel in building relationships, adapting to diverse situations, and providing creative solutions, ensuring personalized and context-aware interactions.

Our ability to handle unusual queries, understand nuances, and offer continuous improvement feedback makes us indispensable in brand communication, where complex, emotional, and nuanced client interactions often require human intervention. Balancing AI automation with the human touch is vital for successful and meaningful brand communication.

Streamlining Administrative Tasks

Administrative tasks, such as data entry, record-keeping, and report generation, are notorious time drains. AI systems can streamline these processes by automating data-related activities. This automation not only reduces the risk of human error but also liberates your time for strategic thinking, client engagement, and brand development.

AI-driven data entry tools can extract information from various sources, including documents, emails, and forms, and populate databases or spreadsheets accurately and efficiently. Additionally, AI can handle data validation and cleansing, ensuring that your data remains accurate and up-to-date. By automating administrative tasks, you can redirect your energy towards initiatives that drive brand growth and innovation.

AI for Customer Insights and Personalization

AI's analytical capabilities extend to deriving actionable insights from vast amounts of client data. By harnessing AI for data analysis, your brand can gain deeper understanding of client behavior, preferences, and trends. This data-driven approach enables your brand to offer personalized experiences that enhance client satisfaction and loyalty.

AI-driven algorithms can segment clients based on their behavior, demographics, and engagement history, allowing your brand to tailor communication and offerings to individual preferences. For example, AI can automate product recommendations, content suggestions, and targeted marketing campaigns. The result is a more engaging and relevant client experience that strengthens client-brand relationships.

Creating a Time Freedom Roadmap

To effectively regain time freedom through AI automation, it is essential to develop a strategic roadmap. This roadmap outlines the specific tasks and processes that can be automated and sets clear milestones for their implementation. It provides a structured approach to gradually reducing time-consuming activities and freeing up your schedule for more strategic and impactful endeavors.

The roadmap should encompass the following key elements:

1. **Task Prioritization:** Identify and prioritize tasks that are ripe for automation, considering their impact on time savings and overall brand efficiency.

2. **Automation Tools:** Select the AI-driven tools and technologies that align with your brand's automation objectives, ensuring that they integrate seamlessly into your existing workflows.

3. **Implementation Timeline:** Define a timeline for the gradual implementation of automation processes, allowing your team to adapt to the changes smoothly.

4. **Monitoring and Optimization:** Establish mechanisms for ongoing monitoring of automated processes and continuous optimization to ensure they deliver the intended results.

5. **Team Training:** Provide training and guidance to your team members to en-

sure they are proficient in working with AI-driven systems and are prepared for their evolving roles.

By creating a well-defined roadmap, your brand can navigate the transition to AI automation systematically and effectively, maximizing the benefits of time freedom.

Balancing Automation with Human Touch

Automation should complement, rather than replace, the human touch in brand communication. It is essential to determine where human interactions hold the greatest value and ensure that AI systems support and enhance these interactions, rather than substituting for them.

Consider scenarios where the personal touch is most meaningful, such as high-stakes client negotiations, complex problem-solving, and empathetic support during challenging times. In such situations, human interactions can build trust, foster deeper client relationships, and convey the brand's commitment to client well-being.

AI should be leveraged to handle routine and repetitive tasks, allowing your team members to focus on high-value activities that require creativity, emotional intelligence, and a personal connection. Striking the right balance between automation and the human touch is essential for maintaining the authenticity and effectiveness of your brand's communication.

In conclusion, regaining time freedom through AI automation is not solely about efficiency; it is about creating space for meaningful client relationships, innovation, and personal growth. As we progress, we will delve deeper into how AI can enhance the client experience in Chapter 11, with a focus on dynamic content and tailored recommendations. This chapter serves as a pivotal step in unlocking the full potential of your brand's communication capabilities.

THOUGHT STARTERS FOR REGAINING TIME FREEDOM WITH AI AUTOMATION

1. **Identifying Time-Consuming Tasks:** List some daily or recurring tasks in your brand communication that you find time-consuming. How do these tasks impact your ability to focus on strategic goals?

2. **Benefits of AI in Project Management:** Discuss the benefits of using AI-based project management and scheduling tools. How can they help you regain control over your schedule and reduce task overload?

3. **Delegating Routine Tasks to AI:** Share examples of routine brand management tasks that can be delegated to AI systems. How can automation improve the efficiency of these tasks?

4. **AI-Enhanced Content Creation:** Explore how AI-powered content generation can streamline your content creation process. How can you maintain content quality while saving time?

5. **Managing Client Engagement at Scale:** Discuss the challenges of maintaining personalized client engagement as your brand grows. How can AI-driven chatbots and virtual assistants assist in this process?

6. **Streamlining Administrative Tasks:** Identify administrative tasks that can be automated using AI. How can automating these tasks free up your time for more strategic activities?

7. **AI for Personalization and Insights:** Share examples of how AI can derive client insights and enhance personalization. How can AI-driven personalization improve the client experience?

8. **Ethical AI Use:** Discuss the importance of ethical AI use in client interactions and automation. How can your brand ensure responsible AI use and data privacy?

9. **Creating a Time Freedom Roadmap:** Develop a roadmap for implementing AI automation in your brand communication. What are the key milestones and tasks to prioritize?

10. **Balancing Automation and the Human Touch:** Reflect on the balance between AI automation and human interactions in your brand communication. Where do you see the greatest value in human touch, and how can AI support these interactions?

11. **Client Feedback on Automation:** Gather feedback from clients about their experiences with AI-driven automation. How has automation impacted their interactions with your brand?

12. **Measuring the Impact of Automation:** Discuss methods for measuring the impact of AI automation on your brand's efficiency, client satisfaction, and overall success.

13. **Overcoming Resistance to Automation:** Explore any resistance within your team or organization to AI automation. How can you address concerns and gain buy-in for automation initiatives?

14. **Future-Proofing with AI:** Consider the evolving landscape of AI technology. How can your brand adapt to new AI advancements to continue regaining time freedom in the future?

These thought starters are designed to stimulate discussions, reflections, and strategic planning related to the integration of AI automation to regain time freedom in brand communication. They can be used in team meetings, workshops, or individual reflections as you explore the practical implications of automation for your brand.

21

MAINTAINING A HUMAN TOUCH WHILE USING AI

Maintaining a human touch while using AI is crucial to ensure that technology enhances rather than replaces human interactions. Here is a list of suggestions to help you strike the right balance:

1. **Personalize AI Interactions:** Configure AI systems to address clients by their names and reference their previous interactions or preferences whenever possible. Personalization fosters a sense of connection.

2. **Transparent AI Use:** Inform clients when they are interacting with AI-powered systems. Transparency builds trust and sets clear expectations.

3. **Empathetic Language:** Train AI systems to use empathetic and compassionate language, especially in sensitive or emotional contexts. Show understanding and support.

4. **Offer a Human Escalation Option:** Always provide an option for clients to connect

with a human representative if they prefer. Ensure that the transition from AI to a human is seamless.

5. **Active Listening:** Encourage AI systems to actively listen to client inquiries and provide thoughtful responses. This demonstrates that their concerns are genuinely considered.

6. **Empower AI to Solve Problems:** Train AI to solve common client issues and provide helpful solutions. Clients appreciate quick problem resolution, whether it's handled by a human or AI.

7. **Maintain Consistency Across Channels:** Ensure that AI-driven communication is consistent with your brand's voice and values across all communication channels, from chatbots to email.

8. **Human Supervision:** Implement human oversight of AI interactions, especially in critical situations or when complex client needs arise. Humans can step in when necessary.

9. **Human-Centric Training:** Train AI systems using human-centric data and insights. The more the AI understands human behaviors and preferences, the more it can mimic a human touch.

10. **Gather and Apply Feedback:** Continuously gather feedback from clients regarding their AI interactions. Use this feedback to refine AI scripts and behaviors to better align with human touch expectations.

11. **Maintain the Personal Touch:** Even in automated responses, include a personal touch when appropriate. For example, express gratitude, wish clients well, or share relevant anecdotes.

12. **Use AI to Enhance Human Interaction:** Implement AI tools that help humans rather than replace them. For example, AI can provide data insights that support more informed human responses.

13. **Review and Audit AI Output:** Regularly review AI-generated content, responses, and interactions to identify and correct any deviations from the desired human touch.

14. **Flexibility in AI Responses:** Ensure that AI systems have the flexibility to adapt

responses based on context. Sometimes, a more informal or friendly tone may be appropriate.

15. **Ethical Considerations:** Adhere to ethical guidelines and regulations when using AI in client communication, especially in data privacy and sensitive topics.

Remember that the goal of AI in client interactions is to enhance the client experience by providing efficient and helpful support while preserving the warmth and personalization associated with human interactions. Continuously assess and refine your AI systems to ensure they align with your brand's values and client expectations.

Reclaim your Precious Time and Dive Into the World of Efficiency!

"AI Automation" is your gateway to optimizing daily routines and unlocking the true potential of artificial intelligence. With our guidance, you'll identify and prioritize tasks that can be automated, stepping onto the path of greater freedom. Download "AI Automation" today and start a journey towards a more productive life, keeping your valuable time for what matters most. Let's embrace the future, together!

standinyourbrandbook.com/aiautomation

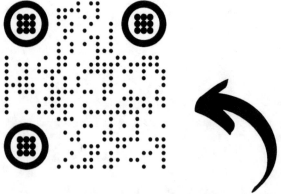

Scan with your phone camera

22

AI-ENHANCED CUSTOMER EXPERIENCE

Exceptional customer experiences lie at the heart of successful brand communication. In this chapter, we delve into the ways AI can elevate the client experience, making it more dynamic, personalized, and tailored to individual needs and preferences.

Dynamic Content and Tailored Recommendations

In the era of personalization, AI emerges as a pivotal tool for delivering dynamic content and tailored recommendations. AI algorithms excel at analyzing client data to suggest products, services, and content that align precisely with each client's interests and behavior.

AI-driven recommendation systems evaluate a plethora of data points, including past purchases, browsing history, demographic information, and real-time interactions. They then generate personalized recommendations that cater to the unique preferences and needs of each client. This level of personalization not only enhances the client experience but also drives increased engagement, conversion rates, and ultimately, client satisfaction.

Enhancing Website and App Experiences

AI extends its personalization capabilities to the digital realm by providing real-time website and app personalization. Whether it involves suggesting relevant content, optimizing navigation, or assisting with searches, AI ensures that every client interaction feels tailored to their individual preferences and objectives.

AI algorithms analyze client behavior, session data, and preferences to dynamically adjust the content and layout of websites and apps. This real-time personalization enhances client engagement, reduces bounce rates, and increases the likelihood of clients finding precisely what they are looking for. The result is an enriched and highly responsive digital experience that leaves clients feeling understood and valued.

Personalized Content and Messaging

AI-driven content personalization takes client communication to the next level. Whether it's emails, newsletters, or marketing campaigns, AI ensures that content and messaging are tailored to individual preferences.

AI analyzes client behavior, engagement history, and content interactions to deliver personalized content recommendations. For instance, AI can determine the most relevant articles to include in a newsletter, suggest product promotions based on past purchases, or customize marketing messages to resonate with specific client segments. This high degree of personalization not only captivates clients but also leads to increased open rates, click-through rates, and conversion rates.

The Role of AI in Brand Differentiation

In an increasingly competitive market, AI-driven customer experiences can become a significant differentiator. Brands that excel in personalized, dynamic interactions stand out and retain loyal clients. AI empowers brands to create memorable experiences that build trust, loyalty, and advocacy.

Differentiating through AI involves consistently delivering exceptional personalized experiences that meet or exceed client expectations. Brands that embrace AI not only retain existing clients but also attract new ones who seek the benefits of tailored, efficient interactions.

AI-Powered Loyalty Programs

Loyalty programs are a powerful tool for client retention, and AI brings them to new heights. By analyzing client behavior and preferences, AI enhances loyalty programs by offering personalized rewards and incentives. AI can predict which incentives are most likely to engage each client, ensuring that loyalty programs are not just generic but truly individualized.

These AI-enhanced loyalty programs foster stronger client-brand relationships. Clients feel recognized and appreciated when they receive rewards that align with their preferences and needs. Additionally, AI can identify optimal points in the client journey to offer these incentives, maximizing their impact on client retention.

Chatbots for Instant Support

AI-driven chatbots serve as invaluable resources for providing instant support around the clock. They are capable of handling routine inquiries, guiding clients through processes, and providing immediate assistance. This ensures that clients always feel attended to, regardless of the time or day.

Chatbots leverage natural language processing and machine learning to understand client queries and provide relevant responses. They can be seamlessly integrated into websites, apps, and messaging platforms, offering clients a convenient and efficient way to seek assistance. By automating these support functions, brands not only enhance client satisfaction but also free up human resources for more complex interactions.

AI-Enhanced Recommendations

Recommendation engines powered by AI are a cornerstone of personalization. These engines analyze a multitude of client data, including past purchases, browsing history, and demographic information, to suggest products or services that align with a client's preferences and needs.

AI-driven recommendations extend beyond simply showcasing related items. They can include personalized bundles, complementary products, and even content recommendations. By tailoring suggestions to individual client profiles, brands increase cross-selling and upselling opportunities, thereby boosting revenue and client engagement.

Predictive Customer Service

AI's predictive capabilities extend to anticipating client service needs before they arise. By analyzing data patterns, AI can alert brands to potential issues, allowing them to proactively address concerns and prevent client dissatisfaction.

For example, AI can predict when a client may encounter technical difficulties based on their usage patterns and send preemptive troubleshooting guides or offer real-time assistance. This predictive approach not only enhances the client experience but also reduces the number of support requests and associated response times. Ultimately, it contributes to higher client satisfaction and loyalty.

Measuring Customer Satisfaction

AI plays a pivotal role in measuring and understanding client satisfaction. By analyzing client feedback, sentiment, and engagement data, AI can provide insights into overall customer satisfaction levels. Brands can use this data to identify areas for improvement and continually enhance the client experience.

AI-driven sentiment analysis tools can categorize client feedback into positive, neutral, or negative sentiments. They can also detect trends and patterns in client comments, allowing brands to pinpoint specific challenges or areas of delight. This data-driven approach empowers brands to make informed decisions that positively impact client satisfaction and loyalty.

Creating a Client-Centric AI Strategy

Developing a client-centric AI strategy is pivotal to leveraging AI for personalization effectively. This strategy should align with your brand's values and goals, ensuring that AI is used to create a seamless and personalized customer journey.

Key components of a client-centric AI strategy include:

1. **Client Understanding:** A deep understanding of client needs, preferences, and challenges serves as the foundation for effective personalization.

2. **Data Collection and Analysis:** Robust data collection and analysis capabilities

are essential for powering AI-driven personalization.

3. **AI Integration:** Seamless integration of AI technologies into client-facing systems and processes is critical.

4. **Continuous Improvement:** Commitment to continually optimizing AI-driven personalization based on client feedback and evolving preferences.

5. **Alignment with Brand Values:** Ensuring that AI-driven personalization aligns with the brand's values and enhances the client experience rather than detracting from it.

In conclusion, AI is a powerful ally in enhancing the client experience. By leveraging AI for personalization, dynamic content, and predictive insights, brands can create memorable interactions that build trust, loyalty, and advocacy. As we progress, we will explore the importance of monitoring and evolving your brand in Chapter 12, ensuring that your brand remains responsive and adaptive in the ever-changing landscape of client expectations and preferences.

THOUGHT STARTERS THAT CAN BE USED FOR AI-ENHANCED

CUSTOMER EXPERIENCE

1. **Personalization in Brand Communication:** Discuss the significance of personalization in modern brand communication. How do personalized experiences impact client satisfaction and loyalty?

2. **Dynamic Content and Recommendations:** Share examples of dynamic content and personalized recommendations you've encountered as a client. How did these experiences influence your perception of the brand?

3. **AI-Enhanced Website and App Experiences:** Explore how AI can improve website and app experiences. What features or functionalities would you expect from a brand that prioritizes personalization?

4. **Personalized Content and Messaging:** Discuss the effectiveness of personalized content and messaging in marketing campaigns. How can brands use AI to tailor messages to individual preferences?

5. **AI-Driven Brand Differentiation:** Explore how AI-driven customer experiences can differentiate brands in competitive markets. Share examples of brands that excel in this regard.

6. **AI-Powered Loyalty Programs:** Discuss the role of AI in enhancing loyalty programs. How can AI-driven rewards and incentives strengthen client retention strategies?

7. **Chatbots for Instant Support:** Reflect on your experiences with AI-driven chatbots in client support. What are the benefits and potential drawbacks of chatbot interactions?

8. **The Impact of AI on Cross-Selling and Upselling:** Share instances where AI-based recommendations influenced your purchasing decisions. How can AI increase sales and revenue for brands?

9. **Predictive Customer Service:** Explore the concept of predictive customer service. How can AI help brands address client concerns before they escalate?

10. **Measuring Customer Satisfaction with AI:** Share experiences or ideas on how AI can measure customer satisfaction and sentiment. What metrics and data sources are valuable for this purpose?

11. **Client-Centric AI Strategy:** Develop a client-centric AI strategy for your brand. How can AI be used to create a more personalized and seamless customer journey?

12. **Client Feedback on AI-Enhanced Experiences:** Gather feedback from clients about their experiences with AI-enhanced customer interactions. What aspects do they appreciate, and what improvements can be made?

13. **AI and Long-Term Client Relationships:** Discuss how AI can contribute to building and maintaining long-term client relationships. How can AI support ongoing client engagement and loyalty?

14. **AI's Role in Client Advocacy:** Explore how AI can influence client advocacy and word-of-mouth referrals. How do exceptional AI-driven experiences encourage clients to become brand advocates?

These thought starters are designed to stimulate discussions, reflections, and strategic planning related to the use of AI in enhancing the customer experience. They can be used in team meetings, workshops, or individual reflections as you explore the practical applications of AI in your brand's interactions with clients.

23

BRAND MONITORING AND EVOLUTION

A brand is not static; it's a living entity that evolves with time and client needs. In this chapter, we delve into the importance of brand monitoring and the strategies needed to ensure your brand remains relevant and resonant with your target audience.

The Dynamic Nature of Brand Communication

Brand communication is far from static; it's a living entity that evolves with time and the ever-shifting landscape of client needs and preferences. In the digital age, where client engagement is ongoing and multidimensional, brand communication must be equally dynamic.

Brand communication involves not only crafting compelling messages but also adapting to changing market dynamics, client preferences, and emerging trends. In this context, AI emerges as an invaluable tool for monitoring, assessing, and evolving your brand's communication efforts.

Utilizing AI Tools for Brand Monitoring

AI offers a treasure trove of powerful tools for brand monitoring, enabling your brand to maintain a vigilant watch over its reputation and impact. These AI tools can tirelessly track brand mentions, perform sentiment analysis, and collect and analyze client feedback across various channels, from social media platforms to customer reviews and beyond.

The insights generated by AI-powered brand monitoring provide your brand with a real-time pulse of its reputation in the digital sphere. It allows you to swiftly respond to emerging issues, capitalize on positive sentiment, and make data-driven decisions to strengthen your brand's positioning and resonance with your target audience.

Assessing Brand Success and Adjustments

In the era of data-driven decision-making, assessing the success of your brand communication efforts is not a luxury but a necessity. AI-generated analytics reports offer comprehensive data on various metrics, including engagement, conversion rates, client satisfaction, and the overall impact of your brand messages.

These reports serve as invaluable compasses, guiding your brand toward informed adjustments and refinements in its communication strategies. By harnessing the power of AI-driven insights, your brand can continually optimize its messaging, content, and engagement tactics to align more closely with the evolving expectations of your audience.

Creating a Long-Term Brand Evolution Plan

Every brand, regardless of its stage of development, must possess the foresight and adaptability to evolve and stay relevant. A long-term brand evolution plan serves as the roadmap that outlines how your brand will adapt to changing client needs, technological advancements, and shifts within your industry.

AI can play a pivotal role in shaping this evolution. By analyzing market trends, client behaviors, and emerging technologies, AI can help your brand anticipate future changes and position itself as an industry leader rather than a follower.

Incorporating Client Feedback and Insights

Clients are a wellspring of valuable insights. Actively gathering feedback, listening to suggestions, and addressing concerns are not only best practices but essential components of an agile brand. AI can amplify the impact of client feedback by analyzing it at scale, identifying trends, and uncovering hidden opportunities for improvement.

By incorporating client feedback and insights into your brand's decision-making processes, you demonstrate a commitment to client-centricity and responsiveness, ensuring that your brand's evolution aligns with the evolving needs and expectations of your valued clients.

Brand Consistency Across All Touchpoints

Maintaining brand consistency is a hallmark of successful brand communication. AI can lend a helping hand in ensuring that your brand's voice, messaging, and visual identity remain consistent across all touchpoints, from websites and social media platforms to email campaigns and offline materials.

By leveraging AI-powered tools for content and brand asset management, your brand can streamline its communication efforts, reduce the risk of inconsistency, and reinforce its identity in the minds of your audience. Consistency is key to building brand recognition and trust.

Monitoring Competitor Activity

In the competitive landscape of brand communication, staying informed about competitor activity is essential. AI tools can be your brand's vigilant eyes and ears in the digital arena, tracking competitor strategies, client engagement, and market trends.

By analyzing data on competitor activity, your brand can gain valuable insights into what works and what doesn't in your industry. Use this intelligence to identify opportunities for differentiation, refine your own approach, and craft communication strategies that set your brand apart.

The Role of Thought Leadership

Positioning your brand as a thought leader in your industry is a potent strategy for maintaining relevance and resonance. AI can empower your brand with the knowledge and insights needed to stay at the forefront of industry trends and innovations.

AI-driven tools can scour vast amounts of data, news, and research to keep your brand updated with the latest developments in your field. Armed with this knowledge, your brand can craft thought-provoking content, share expert opinions, and provide valuable insights to your audience, establishing itself as a trusted source of information.

Case Studies of Brand Evolution

Case studies of brands that have successfully evolved over time offer valuable lessons and inspiration. These real-world examples showcase the strategies and tactics employed by brands that navigated change effectively.

By studying these cases, your brand can gain insights into the challenges and opportunities associated with brand evolution. It can also draw inspiration from the innovative approaches taken by others and apply similar principles to its own journey of adaptation and growth.

Client-Centric Brand Evolution

As your brand evolves, it's paramount to ensure that every step aligns with the evolving needs and expectations of your clients. Your clients should remain at the heart of your brand's evolution, and their satisfaction and well-being should be the compass guiding your decisions.

Consider how your brand can remain client-centric as it grows and adapts. AI can help by analyzing client data and preferences, revealing shifting trends and demands, and informing the client-centric strategies that drive your brand's evolution.

The Ethical Use of AI in Brand Monitoring

Ethical considerations are central to brand monitoring. Your brand must use AI ethically and responsibly, especially in the realm of client data and privacy. AI systems should adhere to strict ethical guidelines, ensuring data privacy, avoiding biases, and upholding transparency in all client interactions.

By championing ethical AI practices, your brand not only maintains client trust but also contributes positively to the responsible use of technology in the industry, setting a standard for ethical conduct.

Staying Ahead of the Curve

In the fast-paced world of brand communication, staying ahead of the curve is a competitive advantage. Rather than merely reacting to changes, your brand can aspire to be a trendsetter, anticipating shifts and proactively adapting its communication strategies.

AI can play a pivotal role in this endeavor by analyzing emerging trends, monitoring client sentiment, and providing early signals of changes in the market. With AI as your strategic ally, your brand can remain agile and responsive, consistently delivering communication that resonates with your audience.

In conclusion, brand monitoring and evolution are integral to maintaining a strong and resilient brand. By harnessing AI tools, actively listening to clients, and staying responsive to market changes, your brand can continue to thrive and meet the evolving needs of your clients. This chapter serves as a compass, guiding your brand toward a future of enduring relevance and resonance.

THOUGHT STARTERS THAT CAN BE USED FOR BRAND MONITORING AND EVOLUTION

1. **The Ongoing Nature of Brand Communication:** Discuss why brand communication is an ongoing process rather than a one-time effort. How does this understanding impact your approach to brand management?

2. **Leveraging AI for Real-Time Brand Monitoring:** Explore the ways AI can assist in real-time brand monitoring. What types of insights can AI tools provide about your brand's online presence?

3. **Measuring Brand Success:** Share key performance indicators (KPIs) that are crucial for measuring the success of your brand communication efforts. How

do you interpret and act on these metrics?

4. **Using AI to Assess Brand Reputation:** Discuss how AI-driven sentiment analysis can help assess your brand's reputation. How can you leverage this data for brand improvement?

5. **Developing a Long-Term Brand Evolution Plan:** Outline the components of a long-term brand evolution plan. What factors should your plan consider, and how can it adapt to changing circumstances?

6. **Incorporating Client Feedback for Brand Improvement:** Share examples of how client feedback has influenced your brand's evolution. How can AI assist in gathering and analyzing this feedback effectively?

7. **Brand Consistency Across Channels:** Discuss the challenges of maintaining brand consistency across various communication channels. How can AI assist in ensuring a unified brand presence?

8. **Competitor Monitoring and Insights:** Explore the benefits of monitoring competitor activity using AI tools. How can insights from competitors inform your brand's strategies?

9. **Thought Leadership and Industry Trends:** Share examples of thought leadership content or initiatives within your industry. How can AI assist in staying updated with industry trends and emerging topics?

10. **Ethical Considerations in AI-Driven Brand Monitoring:** Reflect on the ethical implications of AI in brand monitoring. How can your brand ensure responsible and ethical use of AI in this context?

11. **Case Studies of Brand Evolution:** Analyze case studies of brands that successfully evolved over time. What strategies did they employ, and what lessons can you apply to your brand's evolution?

12. **Client-Centric Brand Evolution:** Explore how your brand can ensure that its evolution remains client-centric. How can you balance client needs with industry trends and technological advancements?

13. **Staying Ahead of the Curve:** Discuss strategies for staying ahead of the curve in your industry. How can your brand be a trendsetter rather than a follower?

14. **Balancing Tradition and Innovation:** Reflect on the balance between preserving your brand's traditional values and embracing innovation. How can your brand evolve while maintaining its core identity?

15. **Continuous Learning and Adaptation:** Share your approach to continuous learning and adaptation in brand communication. How can your brand foster a culture of adaptability?

These thought starters are designed to stimulate discussions, reflections, and strategic planning related to the monitoring and evolution of your brand. They can be used in team meetings, workshops, or individual reflections to help your brand stay agile and responsive in a dynamic market environment.

24

ETHICAL CONSIDERATIONS OF AI IN BRAND COMMUNICATION

In our journey through the transformational potential of AI in brand communication, we've explored the vast opportunities it offers. However, as we stand at the forefront of this digital frontier, it's imperative that we also address the ethical considerations that come hand in hand with the integration of AI into our communication strategies.

The Promise and Responsibility of AI

Artificial Intelligence has undeniably expanded the horizons of brand communication, offering unprecedented opportunities for connection and personalization. However, these capabilities come with an inherent responsibility to uphold ethical standards in the application of AI.

Respecting Client Privacy

Respecting client privacy is paramount in AI-driven brand communication. As brands gather and utilize data to tailor their messaging, safeguarding clients' personal information is non-negotiable. It is necessary to explore and implement strategies that ensure data privacy, include data anonymization, encryption, and transparent data usage policies. These measures prioritize client trust and demonstrate a commitment to responsible data handling.

Transparency and Accountability

Transparency is the cornerstone of ethical AI practices. Clients have the right to know when AI is used in brand communication. Clear communication regarding AI usage is highly important, ensuring clients are aware of how AI enhances their experiences. Accountability, where brands take responsibility for the outcomes of AI-driven decisions, is also highly important and crucially regarded. Addressing any biases within AI algorithms is a crucial aspect of maintaining accountability.

Mitigating Bias in AI Algorithms

AI algorithms, while powerful, can inadvertently perpetuate biases present in the data they are trained on. Recognizing and mitigating bias is essential for ethical brand communication. Explore strategies to identify and rectify bias in AI algorithms, include the role of diverse data sets, algorithmic fairness, and continuous monitoring to ensure fairness and equity.

Data Security and Compliance

Ensuring the security of client data is paramount in AI-driven brand communication. Establishing best practices for data security, including encryption, access control, and vulnerability management is critical for establishing trust.

Compliance with data protection regulations, such as GDPR and CCPA, and how brands can navigate these intricate legal landscapes to safeguard client data and maintain ethical AI practices are of utmost importance to protecting your clients and your brand.

AI and the Human Touch

While AI can enhance brand communication, it should complement rather than replace the human touch. Striking a balance between AI and human interactions is vital for maintaining authenticity and empathy. "AI-augmented" communication, where AI supports human interactions, enables brands to provide personalized experiences while preserving human connection.

Educating Stakeholders

Ethical AI in brand communication requires the collaboration of all stakeholders. It is imperative to emphasize the importance of educating employees, clients, and partners about AI's role and ethical considerations by educating employees, clients, and partners. Transparent AI usage fosters trust and ensures that everyone involved understands both the advantages and limitations of AI in brand communication. Education is the foundation for responsible AI integration.

A Framework for Ethical AI

To conclude this chapter, we will provide a practical framework for ethical AI in brand communication. This framework will encompass fundamental principles, including client consent, transparency, fairness, and ongoing monitoring. It will serve as a guide for brands to navigate the ethical complexities of AI in their communication strategies, empowering them to make ethical decisions that align with their values and client expectations.

In this age of AI, ethics must be the cornerstone upon which we build the future of brand communication. Ethical considerations are not constraints but guiding principles that ensure our brand communication remains responsible, compassionate, and aligned with our values. As we navigate the complex terrain of AI, let us remember that our commitment to ethics will define our brand's legacy.

FRAMEWORK FOR ETHICAL AI IN BRAND COMMUNICATION

1. Client Consent

a. **Informed Consent:** Ensure that clients are well-informed about the use of AI in brand communication. Clearly communicate how AI is utilized, what data is collected, and how it benefits them.

b. **Opt-In Mechanism:** Implement an opt-in system where clients actively agree to AI-driven interactions and personalized experiences.

c. **Granular Control:** Provide clients with the option to control the level of AI involvement in their interactions, allowing them to tailor their experience based on their comfort level.

2. Transparency

a. **AI Disclosure:** Be transparent about the use of AI in brand communication. Clearly state when AI is involved in interactions and how it enhances client experiences.

b. **Data Usage Transparency:** Communicate to clients how their data is collected, stored, and used. Provide a comprehensive privacy policy that is easily accessible.

c. **Explainable AI:** Ensure that AI algorithms used in brand communication are explainable, allowing clients to understand how decisions are made and recommendations generated.

3. Fairness

a. **Bias Mitigation:** Continuously monitor and mitigate bias in AI algorithms to ensure fair treatment of all clients, regardless of their demographic or personal characteristics.

b. **Diverse Data Sets:** Use diverse and representative data sets to train AI algorithms, reducing the risk of biased outcomes.

c. **Algorithmic Fairness:** Implement fairness metrics to evaluate AI algorithms and make necessary adjustments to rectify any disparities.

4. Ongoing Monitoring

a. **Regular Audits:** Conduct regular audits of AI systems to identify and rectify potential issues, including bias, data privacy breaches, or unintended consequences.

b. **Client Feedback Analysis:** Actively listen to client feedback related to AI-driven interactions and use this input to improve AI systems and ensure they align with client expectations.

c. **Compliance Checks:** Stay abreast of evolving data protection regulations and ensure that AI systems comply with the latest legal requirements.

5. Human-AI Collaboration

a. **Complementary Roles:** Define clear roles for AI and human interactions in brand communication. AI should enhance human interactions rather than replace them.

b. **Empathy and Authenticity:** Ensure that AI-augmented interactions maintain a human touch by conveying empathy and authenticity.

c. **Client Support:** Offer easy access to human support for clients who prefer or require personalized assistance beyond AI capabilities.

6. Ethical Leadership

a. **Ethical Guidelines:** Establish and communicate clear ethical guidelines for AI usage within your brand. Ensure that all employees and partners understand and adhere to these guidelines.

    b. **Training and Education:** Continually educate your team and stakeholders on the ethical use of AI, emphasizing its importance and relevance in brand communication.

    c. **Accountability:** Hold individuals and teams accountable for adhering to ethical AI practices, and implement mechanisms for reporting ethical concerns.

7. Client-Centricity

    a. **Client-Centered Design:** Prioritize client needs and preferences in the design and implementation of AI-driven communication strategies.

    b. **Feedback Loop:** Create a feedback loop that enables clients to provide input on AI interactions and suggest improvements.

    c. **Customization:** Allow clients to customize their AI-driven experiences to align with their unique preferences and comfort levels.

This framework provides a structured approach for brands to integrate AI ethically into their communication strategies. By emphasizing client consent, transparency, fairness, ongoing monitoring, human-AI collaboration, ethical leadership, and client-centricity, brands can navigate the ethical complexities of AI while maintaining trust, integrity, and alignment with their values and client expectations.

25

FACT-CHECKING INFORMATION IS ESSENTIAL

Verifying AI-produced content and fact-checking information is essential to ensure accuracy and credibility. Here is a list of resources and tools that can help you in this process:

1.Human Reviewers:

The most reliable method for verifying AI-produced content is to have humans review and fact-check it. This can involve subject matter experts, journalists, or fact-checkers who assess the accuracy of the content.

2. **Fact-Checking Organizations:**

- **Snopes:** A widely recognized fact-checking website that investigates and debunks false claims and misinformation.

- **PolitiFact:** Focused on fact-checking political statements and claims made by public figures.

- **FactCheck.org:** A non-partisan organization that checks the accuracy of political statements in the United States.

3. AI-Enhanced Fact-Checking Tools:

- **ClaimBuster:** An AI tool that identifies factual claims within text and helps fact-check them.

- **TruthNest:** An AI-powered fact-checking platform that assesses the credibility of news articles and social media posts.

4. **News Outlets and Journals:** Reputable news outlets often have fact-checking departments. Cross-referencing information with established news sources can help verify accuracy.

5. **Academic Research:** Academic papers and research studies can provide in-depth information and data to verify claims and content.

6. **Google Search:** Conducting a web search to see if multiple sources corroborate or dispute the information in question can be a valuable fact-checking method.

7. **Wikipedia:** While not a primary source, Wikipedia often contains citations and references that can lead to reliable information.

8. AI Fact-Checking Tools:

- **AI2's ClaimBuster:** A tool that can be used to automatically identify factual claims within text.

- **ClaimReview Schema:** A schema developed by Schema.org that allows search engines to display fact-checking information alongside search results.

9. **Government and NGO Websites:** Government websites and non-governmental organizations often publish accurate and fact-checked information on various topics.

10. **Social Media Monitoring Tools:** Tools like CrowdTangle or TweetDeck can

help monitor social media conversations and track the spread of information, enabling fact-checking efforts.

11. **Library Resources:** Libraries can provide access to books, journals, and databases that can aid in verifying information.

12. **Cross-Referencing:** Cross-reference information across multiple reliable sources to ensure consistency and accuracy.

Remember that fact-checking can be a time-consuming process, but it's crucial for maintaining the credibility and reliability of information in an age where AI-generated content can sometimes be misleading. Utilizing a combination of these resources and methods can help ensure the accuracy of AI-produced content.

Embrace the Power of Informed Discernment!

In a world brimming with digital content, discerning the real from the artificial is crucial. Introducing "Verify AI-Produced Content," your essential toolkit for navigating the ever-evolving digital landscape. Equip yourself with the knowledge and tools to fact-check and verify AI-generated materials effectively. Ensure the authenticity and trustworthiness of the content you consume and create. Download now and step into a future of confident, credible digital interaction.

standinyourbrandbook.com/verifyAI

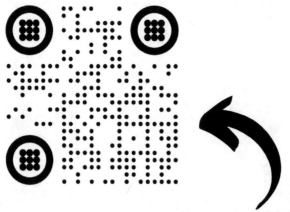

Scan with your phone camera

26

CONCLUSION: NAVIGATING THE FUTURE OF BRAND COMMUNICATION WITH AI

As we conclude this journey through the intricacies of brand communication in the age of AI, it's clear that the landscape of branding is undergoing a profound transformation. You have been guided through the essential principles of connecting with clarity, confidence, and compassion in brand communication, all while embracing the incredible potential of artificial intelligence.

In each chapter, we've explored the ways AI can empower your brand to create deeper connections, streamline processes, and enhance the client experience. From the foundational understanding of brand identity to the dynamic realm of AI-driven personalization, we've witnessed how technology can be a catalyst for growth and innovation.

The chapters have illuminated the importance of:

- **Brand Foundations:** Crafting a strong identity that resonates with your values, mission, and vision.

- **AI-Driven Research:** Leveraging AI tools for market analysis, trend tracking, and consumer insights.

- **Clarity in Brand Messaging:** Ensuring that your brand communicates with precision and authenticity.

- **AI in Content Creation:** Using AI to craft compelling narratives and resonate with your audience.

- **Pricing Strategies:** Optimizing your offerings and pricing through AI-powered analysis.

- **Rebranding with Confidence:** Navigating the rebranding process with AI for brand consistency.

- **Building Trust and Authority:** Using AI-generated social proof and insights to build client trust.

- **AI in Brand Automation:** Streamlining communication and support through chatbots and virtual assistants.

- **Data-Driven Decisions:** Leveraging AI for data analytics to drive brand growth.

- **Regaining Time Freedom:** Harnessing AI to automate tasks and focus on strategic goals.

- **AI-Enhanced Client Experiences:** Creating dynamic, personalized, and client-centric interactions.

- **Brand Monitoring and Evolution:** Adapting your brand to stay relevant and responsive.

- **Ethical Considerations of AI in Brand Communication:** Upholding ethical standards in the application of AI.

Throughout this journey, we've emphasized that AI is not a replacement for human touch but a powerful complement. It's a tool that can help you connect with your clients on a deeper level, understand their needs, and offer tailored solutions. AI allows you to reclaim time, automate routine tasks, and invest in the relationships that matter most.

As the world of brand communication continues to evolve, remember that it's not just about adopting the latest technology but about staying true to your brand's values and the principles. By balancing the capabilities of AI with the human touch, you can create brand experiences that resonate, inspire, and endure.

As a leader in brand communication and early adopter of AI, I encourage you to embrace AI as a partner in your brand's journey. Continue to learn, adapt, and innovate, for the future holds limitless possibilities for those who dare to navigate the ever-changing seas of branding with clarity, confidence, and compassion.

May your brand continue to thrive, connect, and make a lasting impact in the lives of your clients and the world.

AN INVITATION TO IMPLEMENTATION

Dear reader,

I invite you to explore the transformative "Stand in Your Brand" course. This comprehensive course not only provides you with practical how-to instructions but also offers personalized guidance on implementing and embracing AI as a pivotal part of your brand communications strategy. Whether you're looking to streamline your processes, deepen your understanding of your ideal clients, or enhance your brand's impact, this course equips you with the tools and knowledge to do so effectively. Don't miss the opportunity to harness the power of AI and elevate your brand communication to new heights. Visit 30secondsuccess.com/courses today and embark on a journey toward brand success.

Wishing you much success,

Laura T.

ACKNOWLEDGMENTS

To my Lord and Savior, Jesus Christ. Your divine inspiration and wisdom have guided these words, and I am but a vessel for your message. Thank you for guiding me on this wonderous journey to serve others.

To my beloved husband, you are the anchor of my past, the joy of my present, and the promise of our future. With you, I can conquer anything life presents. I love you always and forever. LUMAMED!

To my cherished children and precious grandchildren, you fill my heart with boundless joy and wonder. I am profoundly blessed by your love, and I hold you close in my heart. I love you as big as the world!

To my parents who have always believed in me. Thank you, Mom, for the love and support you've provided throughout my entire life. And to you in heaven Dad, I still hear you. I love you both!

An extra special shout-out to my incredible accountability partners, coaches, mentors, and clients who continuously challenge me and ignite my inspiration to serve with more clarity, confidence, and compassion.

To the dedicated team that brought this book to life (including the remarkable ChatGPT team and the visionary minds behind OpenAI), together, we are an unstoppable force, and I am profoundly grateful for your contributions.

And to you, dear reader, thank you for placing your trust in my work. May you always move forward with hope and find the guidance you seek to serve with joy and purpose.

AUTHOR BIO: LAURA TEMPLETON

Laura Templeton is a dynamic figure in the world of brand communication, hailing from the charming Bucks County, Pennsylvania, USA and currently making her home in the sunny haven of Bradenton, Florida, USA. Armed with a degree in Interior & Exterior Design/Project Management, Laura embarked on a diverse career journey that saw her spend a decade in Corporate Property Management before a pivotal transition.

With the birth of her first child, Laura gracefully transitioned into the role of family manager, stepping into the shoes of a part-time direct sales leader and team trainer after the birth of her second child. Her 15-year foray into the professional arena took an exciting turn when she assumed the role of National Director for the Professional Women's Business Network. It was during this tenure that Laura encountered the common challenge among her members: crafting a brand message that truly resonated and could be delivered in 30 seconds or less with clarity and confidence.

Driven by a passion to assist business owners in overcoming the struggles of effective brand communication, Laura founded her venture, 30 Second Success, in 2015. With a desire to reach a larger audience she worked diligently to receive her certificate from Heroic Public Speaking Graduate School, finishing in early 2020. Quickly embracing the online space for delivering her inspiring talks to a worldwide audience.

Laura continuously receives accolades for speaking to groups and organizations and she was recently voted Alignable Small Business of the Year in 2022 & 2023, a testament to her dedication. Laura is also the bestselling author of "30 Second Success: Ditch the Pitch & Start Connecting!" and a contributing author to the acclaimed book "Your First Year: What I Wish I'd Known" and currently has 2 more anthologies ready for release.

An early adopter of AI, Laura continues to be a driving force in the world of brand communication. She is determined to teach audiences and clients to leverage AI for better brand communications and time reclamation. Her latest endeavor, "Stand In Your Brand: Harness the Power of AI for Brand Success, Efficiency, and Client Attraction," is aimed at empowering others to communicate their brands effectively, reclaim their time, and attract more clients in the online and offline space.

Beyond her professional pursuits, Laura is a dedicated wife, a loving mother, a proud grandmother, and a devoted rescue dog mom. She thrives in the great outdoors, indulging her love for biking, hiking, and any opportunity to be near the water. As a certified USA Archery Instructor, she finds joy in precision and target shooting, further illustrating her zest for mastering the art of communication, whether with bows or words.

Connect with Laura on LinkedIn, Facebook, Instagram, and YouTube:

@30secondsuccess

Visit Laura's website https://30secondsuccess.com

OTHER BOOKS BY LAURA TEMPLETON

Get them wherever books are sold!

30 Second Success: Ditch the pitch and start connecting!

The book contains a step-by-step process and all the tools you'll need to write - and share - your thirty second message with clarity and confidence. Having the 30 Second Success Formula™ and other networking strategies in your toolkit will help you increase referrals, grow your business, and become the master connector you're meant to be.

Your First Year: What I Wish I'd Known

Lessons from Women entrepreneurs for Women Entrepreneurs. The generous and hard-won wisdom in this book won't cure-all, but it will reassure you that following your internal GPS is just as (or maybe more) important as getting advice. The women authors in this book want you to succeed. They're cheering you on as you make an impact in Your First Year...and beyond!